# THE REAL ESTATE INVESTING DIET

**www.amplifypublishing.com**

*The Real Estate Investing Diet:*
*Harnessing Health Strategies to Build Wealth in Ninety Days*

**For more information, please contact:**
Amplify Publishing, an imprint of Mascot Books
620 Herndon Parkway, Suite 320
Herndon, VA 20170
info@amplifypublishing.com

Library of Congress Control Number: 2021912818
CPSIA Code: PRV0222A
ISBN-13: 978-1-64543-857-1

Printed in the United States

To those who came before us and allowed us to have a dream, and to the ones who proved that dreams are real—all we have to do is just believe.

*"If you want to be great at something, there's a choice you have to make. What I mean by that is, there are inherent sacrifices that come along with that. Family time, hanging out with friends, being a great friend, being a great son, nephew, whatever the case may be."* –Kobe Bryant

*"We don't decide our future, we decide our habits, and our habits decide our future. The power of a habit can control your destiny."*
–Myles Munroe

# The
# REAL
# ESTATE
## Investing Diet

Harnessing
Health Strategies
to Build Wealth
in Ninety Days

## ANDRÉ STEWART

amplify

# CONTENTS

# INTRODUCTION

MANY PEOPLE HAVE TRIED or at least read about some type of diet. Whether or not they finally achieved the desired results is the difference. The diet plan that you're being provided is like any other diet plan; results will vary from person to person. We all know that diets do work if they are followed step by step. This particular real estate diet I know works effectively. After seven months of being on it, I increased my net worth in real estate to over $1.2 million, and achieved that feat without using my own money. I'm 100 percent positive that if you follow the principles and diet outlined in this book, you will not only get rich with real estate, but it will translate to success anywhere you apply these principles and the results can be achieved which will allow you to quit your job in ninety days or less.

In *The Real Estate Investing Diet,* I'm going to simplify how to build a net worth of a million dollars and more. I'm also going to give you simple strategies to supplement your income with real estate, just by applying the same principles as you would on a simple diet.

In case you're wondering if you can achieve this ("Perhaps this diet is meant for only rich people?"), let me share my story with you. I grew up in poverty between two households, my parents and my grandparents on my mother's side. When living with my grandparents, we received government assistance in the form of food stamps, food and housing. Government assistance would occasionally drop off food which seemed to be made of god knows what—the peanut butter wouldn't spread on bread, the cheese wouldn't melt at 400 degrees. (Anyone who has grown up in poverty will definitely recognize this and may be thinking, *Oh yeah!*)

My parents were both military officials, trying to raise two kids while making under $27,000 a year. My father had other kids before he met my mother that he was also supporting, so money was scarce in both environments. As I got older, I remember my mom saying, "Sometimes I would spend my last just to take you guys to McDonalds on Fridays." As a kid, you don't understand how real the struggle is for the people taking care of you.

Most of my time growing up was spent in the Midwest and the South, so I dealt with a lot of prejudice and racism. Growing up in environments like this, you don't have a lot of options or a lot of great role models, so you head down some wrong paths. By the time I was eight, I had already committed to getting myself and my family out of that situation by any means necessary. Based on my surroundings, I was convinced that either selling drugs and or basketball was the way to get my family out of these situations.

By the time I was 19, I had three near-death experiences, one at point-blank range, hearing a bullet whizzing past my ear. Nonetheless, my fuel and life's purpose was to get rich and help my family out. I was continuously saying, "I'm going to be a millionaire." I had even come up with two businesses by the time I was 16. The first was landscaping; for the other, I partnered with a recreation center to create a teen center where kids could hang out on the weekends to avoid the street life. Later on in life, I tried selling Herbal Life, MonaVie, other MLMs and a host of other things but needless to say, none of them worked out.

Around age 24, I started reading books on how the rich think, yet I didn't have the mindset, plan, or vehicle. At age 32, I discovered real estate, and got a mentor who made over $10 million in real estate, and gave me his system. Less than two years after I found the right vehicle known as real estate, I built my net worth in just residential real estate to $1.2 million and overall net worth of $12 million.

Around that time, I also founded the global real estate investing app InvestFar, as well as an online real estate investing and business education platform called Residual Roads Business Institute.

I didn't let my past experiences or upbringing dictate the outcome of my future. Instead, I became the opposite of what statistics said I should have become. On my way, the amount of obstacles that I had to face ranged from law enforcement harassment, racism, near-death experiences, gang violence, severe depression, homelessness, eviction, government assistance, a torn Achilles tendon...I could keep going, but the fact is that I was relentless in my pursuit, as you have to be. We all have a list of experiences that shape our belief system; some of yours could be less or greater than mine. Don't let the past or your current circumstances dictate your future. Always remember, your situation is only temporary, if you want it to be.

## Before You Begin

As you start to read this book, please do not touch anything related to real estate until you have completed the steps in the first two chapters. Being successful or rich is not luck; it requires you to do what successful people do, and being coachable and disciplined are two of the most important traits you must have.

Another important trait is productive habits—if you tell me your habits, I can tell you your future. Habits control where we end up on our journey as it dictates why we do the things we do in regards to life, finances and business. Your ability to be successful on this diet and achieve the desired results may require you to adopt new productive habits and delete or break bad habits. Most successful people have more productive behavioral habits such as reading a certain amount per day or a number of books in a week, exercising 3-4 times a week, not checking their phone the first hour of the day, or creating protected time every day for a particular goal. They also know how to keep their thoughts in a positive state which in turn produces more action or activity conducive to their success. Productive habits by nature should always put you in an environment to win and this is even more so if built on a proper foundation. Having a proper foundation is a must if this is the journey you're seeking. For example, if a house is built on a rocky foundation, what happens with the home? It's unstable. Even if the house has been standing for years, at some point the house will have to be restructured, or it may collapse. No one has ever built wealth being unstable. Even athletes or actors didn't wake up in the pros or as celebrities; they put in the work early to get to the top. I ask that you allow me to break apart your foundation, but I promise to rebuild you on solid ground.

You're reading this, so a part of you wants something different. To do that, please promise to participate at 100 percent while on this diet to achieve those desired results. Why pick up the book and start the diet if you're going to half-ass it?

Trust me when I say that on the real estate investing diet, you can and will achieve the same result (if not better) than other millionaire investors if you follow the plan step by step. Like any diet, the results depend on you!

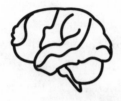

# CHAPTER 1

# MENTAL CONDITIONING

THERE IS ONE THING all successful people share, whether it's a star athlete such as Kobe Bryant, a successful business owner like Bill Gates, or a real estate investor like Grant Cardone who has made millions. That one thing is mental conditioning. This is the most important part of not only becoming a million-dollar real estate investor, but for success in your everyday walk of life.

A famous quote comes to mind when I think of the mentality that most successful people share, one that I have lived life by since my early twenties. It was said by one of the most winning coaches in NFL history, the late great Vince Lombardi:

*"The quality of a person's life is in direct proportion to their commitment to excellence, regardless of their chosen field or endeavor."*

When I think about this quote, it brings to mind a mantra

which holds true to all things: *"How you do anything is how you do everything."*

We all have people in our lives that come to mind when we think about something being done half-assed. Take a minute and pull this person into focus—could it be you? Think about what you've witnessed them do with little effort or care. Now visualize other areas of their life—did it carry over? The answer is probably a resounding *yes*, and the reason is that our brains usually operate on default mode.

There are two ways that our brain functions. One is the default mode, where we mentally condition ourselves to operate a certain way in most things we do. That's how some people can drive home from work while texting, only glancing at the road periodically. They've done this routine so many times that they don't have to stay present in the process.

Direct mode is when we are in the moment and focused, dodging a possible car accident because we are present and seeing things before they come. I am certain that highly successful people stay in the direct mode more than on autopilot, which is what makes them great. They make the commitment to excellence, and never switch to autopilot, because that leads to being in comfort zones with lackluster results. Life begins at the end of our comfort zone. This chapter may make you uncomfortable, but on the other side of discomfort, there's growth.

*"People do shit that is comfortable and make excuses for anything that makes them uncomfortable because that's easier."* We should all want to thrive in discomfort, as it makes everything outside of it that much easier. Always remember that you can't improve without change. Take a moment and think about a time in life when you made a commitment to raise a standard

in an area of your life, and that part of your life changed. You had to step out of your comfort zone in that aspect of your life to activate that change.

## Changing Your Mental Conditioning

Did you know change happens in an instant? In a split-second, your life can be completely different. A car accident last about 30 seconds or less, but what happens to the victims lasts much longer. Say a person was 30 years old and they have been driving since they were 16. Now, all of a sudden, 14 years of their life don't matter; they are mentally conditioned to never want to drive again because of something that happened in 30 seconds. That's how important mental conditioning is.

The majority of people are mentally conditioned by their circumstances: their upbringing, the neighborhood they grew up in, etc. Some of us have stronger mental conditioning, or weaker mental conditioning. Individual experiences in life or by educating yourself on a particular subject can increase mental conditioning as you will either know what to expect because you have been through it or you have been trained so you know what you're looking for. Navy SEALS are known to be the toughest people mentally on earth and it's due to the amount of immense pressure they are put under physically and mentally during their training. When a SEAL shows up regardless of the situation you know they will get the task done by any means necessary or they will lose their life trying.

In any endeavor, there's a certain level of relentlessness you must have on the path to being successful. When it comes to real estate investing, your first deal may not come for two years.

If you don't have the mental conditioning to withstand losing deals because of lack of funding, missed opportunity, or because the seller backed out and went with another buyer, you will not make it as a real estate investor.

If your first thought is, "Maybe he is right; I wonder if I should give up?", you should stop reading this book right now, because you've already given in to the outside noise. Most people don't succeed because of naysayers, people telling them they can't do it, or they are going to fail. One thing that successful people have mentally conditioned themselves to know is that failure is necessary; if you're not failing, that means you're not trying.

What I want you to do is reframe the way you look at failures. Look at failure as a seminar, where you have attained some sort of knowledge or skill that you will take with you forever.

If you fail on a deal and it cost you $9,000, don't think, "Oh man, I just lost $9,000." Think of it this way: "That was an expensive seminar, but I learned a lot, and I won't pay that much again." Reframing is an essential tool in the process of mental conditioning, and you can use it in any area of your life. If you reframe the way you see negative things, you are more likely to become not only a successful real estate investor, but also a better person.

Another part of being prepared mentally is to understand that seeds that are planted when you're learning the process of becoming a real estate investor, and you have to give those seeds some time to sprout. If you expect to jump in and land a sweet deal as soon as you are done reading this book, let me break it down for you: it won't be as easy as the book makes it seem.

This is the reason why you hear so many real estate investors say, "It took me almost two years to get my first deal." Starting out, most people don't have the connections, the financing or the resources to purchase their first investment property. This is where mental conditioning plays a huge part in staying with the diet. A lot of people on traditional diets give up after a week or two of not seeing any results. On this diet it will be no different, so you have to be mentally prepared to possibly not see results for the first two or three weeks. The good thing is that the further along you get in this book, the higher the probability that you will see quicker results, as I provide step-by-step strategies for accelerated results.

Again, when seeds are planted, they take time to sprout. There's a story of a man who planted a bamboo tree. Every day around 5:30 a.m., he would go outside and water the seed in the ground.

One day, his neighbor came over and said, "I've been watching you water this patch of dirt almost a year now and nothing's grown. You should probably just give up, because it was probably a bad seed." The guy looked at the neighbor and smiled and said, "Thanks, but I'm going to keep watering it." The neighbor walked off and said, "You're crazy, man." But the guy watering the bamboo seed knew something that the neighbor didn't. He knew that a bamboo seed takes at least five years before it sprouts, but as soon as it breaks through the ground, within 60 days the bamboo tree will be 10 feet tall. He was mentally conditioned and committed to watering this seed every single day, because he knew what the benefits would be once it sprouted. What do you think happened when the neighbor saw his 10-foot bamboo tree in 45 days? He saw a man watering a patch of dirt for 5 years straight consistently with no change, and then all of a sudden, the fruits of his neighbor's labor were so substantial that anyone passing by could see.

You have to be relentless on this diet, and in any other areas of your life that you want to change.

Basketball is another example of how important mental conditioning is. My high school basketball coach, Victor Joyner, was a great coach. We won conference championships year after year, had undefeated runs, and could outrun any team placed in front of us. One of the main reasons is because Coach Joyner didn't let us touch a basketball for at least the first six weeks of the new season. All we did was run! Stairs, line drills, two-mile jogs, weight training, and then run some more. By the time we touched a basketball, we were so conditioned that we could practice for two hours straight, day after day, and never feel exhausted. When it was time to do skill drills, we could do them forever because we never got tired, and we were able to develop faster in a shorter period of time. In games, we were unstoppable, and our skill set could last into overtime if needed. Real estate investing will always take you into overtime, so you have to be prepared.

"Mamba mentality," as Kobe Bryant called it, is about obsession. It is about prioritizing your professional goals over having a normal, balanced life. It is about playing without fear, mastering your craft and wanting not only to win, but to dominate in your chosen field or endeavor. This is something that I had before he coined the term. One of the reasons Kobe Bryant was one of mine and many other people favorite player and silent mentor is because those with that mentality are cut from the same cloth in our approach to life and business. I was fortunate to be at the game against Golden State April 13th, 2013 when Kobe tore his Achilles. Steph Curry had 53, but it wasn't enough as Kobe was in "Mamba mode," pushing my beloved Lakers to the playoffs. Up until that point, I couldn't remember or knew anyone tearing their Achilles. After seeing Kobe fall 7 times, I told my friend Mark, "He needs to slow down." Three plays later, Kobe ruptured his Achilles. To this day, there has never been another player to rupture an Achilles in basketball and walk of their own will to the free-throw line to hit two free throws to seal a win.

That is the type of relentless mental toughness you need to become a successful real estate investor and quit your job in 90 days or less. Like Coach Joyner would say, *"Basketball is 70 percent mental and 30 percent physical."* The same goes for the realm of success. 80 percent of success is psychological, and 20 percent is mechanics.

You also have to set standards for yourself. Most people's standards are to pay their bills, and they don't believe they can meet this standard without having a job. Wants don't get met, but standards do. Mentally condition yourself to have higher standards, for yourself and for the people around you, as well. You are an average of the five people you hang out with, and the same rule applies to income. If you want a higher income, surround yourself with successful investors or business owners who are on the same "diet" and can keep you accountable.

CHAPTER 2

# LIMITING BELIEFS

UNTIL 1954, NO ATHLETE had ever run a mile in under four minutes. Everyone said it was physically impossible, until one day Roger Bannister broke that barrier. He wasn't a star athlete— he attained this record with minimal training, while practicing as a doctor. What did he do differently? How could a regular, everyday man become the first person to do the "impossible?" He had a mental shift, a change in his mind. He believed he could, so he did.

Bannister's record lasted just for 46 days. Within two years, 37 people ran a four-minute mile, and since then, over 20,000 people have done it. It took just one person's action to shift the entire belief system of thousands of people.

## Change Your Beliefs, Change Your Brain

In the previous chapter, I mentioned that I was at the Lakers game where Kobe ruptured his Achilles. Exactly six months later, I ruptured mine in a game, I recall the entire incident. The first two quarters I was not playing explosively because the gym was cold and I didn't feel confident enough yet to go full force. Around halftime I felt my body start to loosen up and thought to myself, *Okay, it's time.* I caught. the ball on the wing by the three-point line to make a move to drive past my defender and as soon as I exploded off my right foot, pop! I fell to the ground, the whistle blew, a foul was called, I looked behind me to see if someone kicked me but it was only the referee standing on the baseline, that is when I knew I ruptured my Achilles. I witnessed and heard Kobe tell his story so that immediately came to mind. But trust me, I didn't even think about shooting free throws. However, I did sit on the sidelines and watch our team finish the game; it was a mandatory win to make it to playoffs, and had I asked one of my teammates to take me to the hospital, we would have had to forfeit.

I believed I could sit there, muscle through the pain, finish the game and have a good recovery because my favorite player did it. After the game, I went to the ER and shortly afterward, I began my journey of learning how to walk again. As hard of a hill this was to climb, I believed I could do it because Kobe did it. Thanks to a friend who works for the Lakers, Kobe actually gave me a pair of his shoes to recover in. This made me believe even more in my recovery!

I gained 20 pounds during this time since I couldn't work out. I didn't like the way I felt or looked, and my jeans fit tighter, but I refused to buy new clothes. What did I do instead? Diet!

Millions of people are dying because of what they're eating, but more people are dying because of what's eating them. Most people's daily diet consists of Instagram, Facebook, news, and things that fuel their negative beliefs. Even though being an entrepreneur or a real estate investor is a trend right now because of social media, most people won't be successful because they don't actually believe they can. They were taught that money is evil, that you need money to make money, that rich people are bad, and "the man" is holding them back.

If this is what you believe, it will always be the case for you. You can only produce what your brain thinks you're capable of.

For example, have you ever noticed how once you buy a specific car, you see that car everywhere? They have always been there, but you have made your brain aware, so now its filter (called the reticular activator) is searching to produce what you have programmed it to do. Real estate investing is the same. Once you believe you can become an investor and you have mentally conditioned your mind, programmed it, and made it aware, its job now is to produce results of what it is you're searching for.

## Stretching

Think of a rubber band. How does it grow? You have to apply tension between two points. When the tension is not there, it doesn't stretch and grow.

Your belief system works the same way. For you to believe you can do a thing that you haven't done before, you have to step out in faith and stretch your thinking to believe that you can do what you've never done before. Don't limit yourself based on beliefs that were anchored in you by past experiences, by your upbringing or people you hang out with.

Furthermore, when you stop stretching for the wrong things, then you allow the right things to help you grow. Here is a list of eight things I suggest that you give up, if you want to grow.

1. Give up worrying about the past and start focusing on your future. Life is not promised. Think about what has ever actually changed in a situation by worrying about it.
2. Let go of waiting. What you don't start now will never get started. Procrastination equals stagnation. Slow progress is still progress.
3. Stop trying to be everything for everyone. You will not and cannot make everyone happy. It's that simple—don't even try.
4. "I can't" is no longer in your vocabulary. As Henry Ford said, "Whether you think you can, or you think you can't, either way you are right."
5. No more complaining. Get it done, by any means necessary or figure out a solution.
6. Do not compare yourself to others. We are all unique individuals in our own right, even identical twins. The only person to measure yourself against is you.
7. Give up focusing on what you don't want to happen. You bring about what you think about.
8. Stop avoiding risk. This is the only way you will be successful in real estate investing.

Take a moment and write 10 negative beliefs that stopped your growth:

_____

_____

_____

_____

_____

_____

_____

_____

_____

> *"As a man thinks, so is he"* –*Proverbs 23:7*

People that have become wealthy from real estate investing think differently about money than the majority. Most people look for ways to spend money as soon as they get a raise or a tax return; it's almost like it burns a hole in their pocket. Wealthy people, on the other hand, look for ways to invest any money beyond their expenses.

Most people think that if they get a better job and higher pay, they will get rich one day. Wealthy people know that a job will never make them rich; only investing will.

Most people think if they invest a little money, they can somehow get a miraculous return. Wealthy people know that more zeros equal a high profit on an investment return.

Most people stay away from risk because they think they might fail. Wealthy people know that if they don't take any risks, they've already failed.

What would you do if you knew you couldn't fail?

## Core Beliefs

Everyone looks at the world differently. Two people may have the same experience yet have very different interpretations of what happened. Core beliefs are the deeply held beliefs that influence how we interpret our experiences.

Think of core beliefs like a pair of glasses. Everyone has a different perception that causes them to see things differently. For example, when you meet a person and want to ask them out to dinner, your core beliefs may say, "I don't look good today" or "I'm not good enough for them." The result is that you don't ask that person out who could have been your soulmate. As a kid my dad would always tell me don't be afraid to ask a person out, worse they can do is tell you no and you never know if they could be the one. As he told me about the story of how he met my mother, even though my mother was shy and not very talk-ative he asked her out and 39 years later they are still together. Had he not asked her to dinner I would not be here today.

Negative core beliefs cause consequences.

Up above, you identified and wrote down at least 10 negative core beliefs. Now let's begin to challenge them.

List at least three scenarios that are contrary to the negative beliefs you listed.

Although we may be unaware of these negative beliefs, the good news is that they are completely false. Core beliefs are simply patterns that you repeat throughout your life until you can reframe or balance them out to a positive pattern. A core belief is always an internal representation of what a person thinks of themself. A supporting belief is a prediction for a forecast in your mind about what others will do or have done to you. Many people hold onto negative belief patterns, which leads to thoughts that are counterproductive to being successful. Thoughts or ideas may seem to reside in your mind, but in reality, each thought exists as a wave of energy called a thought-form. Energy flows where your attention goes, so it is important to make sure you're always in a positive state and thinking about what you're looking to accomplish, not the opposite.

Most successful real estate investors are abundant thinkers—they think big and are always positive. While a person who thinks from a viewpoint of lack will panic if values drop in a home, an abundant thinker would say, "Even if the value drops, it will always rebound if I don't sell."

The key is always thinking with abundance. You can only go where your thoughts take you.

## Recognizing Your Own Abundance

One of the keys to abundance is being aware of how much we're always supported. When a negative belief arises, remember the times you received support from expected and unexpected sources. What I think when times get tough (and trust me, they will get tough, even once you become wealthy in real estate) is that it always works out.

Stay in a state of gratitude. The most difficult time to do this is when you are in a bad situation or feeling less of yourself. Many of us have experienced being in the red financially, but some feel broke even with having millions of dollars in the bank. This means their mental state is in lack, and that is the opportune time to get into a state of abundance or gratitude. Again, energy flows where the attention goes.

## Now Is the Time

The time to thrive is now. Not tomorrow, or sometime in the future—now.

Having a vision for a future that differs from your current situation is inspiring and exciting. It also keeps you from committing to your present position. Many people have dreams and goals for a lifestyle that they wish to live, but limiting beliefs hold them people back from reaching their desired outcome. They may feel that they have to hold back on the lifestyle they want because they don't want to leave people behind, or because of what was taught to them as a child. What is actually happening is that they are afraid to embrace change—they fear that reaching their desired outcome will mean cutting people off or losing friends and loved ones. This belief creates a tendency for people to hold back from fully pursuing their passion.

As humans, we have patterns that prevent us from committing ourselves to create the life we deserve. There are no guarantees in life, so not pursuing your life's purpose puts you at risk of the world not receiving your individual gifts.

If you have many limiting beliefs, work on creating a new neurological pathway that is automatic in producing positive thoughts. A dirt pathway in the woods wasn't created by the city—it was created by someone trying to get from point A to point B, either in a shorter distance or to get to the top of a mountain. Create your own path. Don't let the limiting beliefs laid out by family members, friends or past experiences determine the journey you take. For you to achieve success in real estate investing, you have to believe you can.

CHAPTER 3

# DIET PLAN PREPPING

ON ANY DIET, YOU have to plan your day or week around tracking your food intake. For example, don't eat after 6 p.m., eat five to six times per day, drink two protein shakes per day, etc. To be effective, people have to be disciplined and use a tracker, app or calendar to achieve the desired outcome.

That rule is extremely important on this diet, as well. Before real estate investing was my way of life, I had real estate "power hours" in my phone calendar. An alarm would go off, reminding me to complete a real estate-related task. The task could range from finding leads to sending out mailers, finding a free seminar, or scouring Zillow for properties. In real estate investing, it's important to stay on a learning track every day in the first 30 days to create crucial habits.

If you have a corporate or an office environment job, I'm pretty sure you actively use your calendar, especially in a sales position. Real estate investing is majority sales, and you're selling yourself constantly, whether it be at a meetup, REIC, or raising funds to buy deals, so it's important never to be late, miss a call or a meeting, and to stay on a learning track every day in the first 30 days to create crucial habits. A successful real estate investing diet should consist of understanding the different facets of real estate, exit strategies, sales, and which area you want to focus on out of the four types of real estate.

| Days\| Weeks | 1 | 2 | 3 | 4 |
|---|---|---|---|---|
| SUN | ☐ Learning Day! Invest 2 Hours -- Real Estate podcast session. | ☐ Find Property Leads Use Zillow or a list source for lead generation for your business. | ☐ Learning Day! Invest 3 Hours -- Real Estate podcast session or YouTube videos. | ☐ Build Buyers List Sign up for Meetup groups or REI Clubs and network with members. |
| MON | ☐ Discovery Monday! Find out what your potential clients are looking for. Send 50 emails to leads. | ☐ Social Hashtag Share a post using Monday's hashtag. | ☐ Discovery Monday! Find out what your potential clients are up to. Send 30 emails to leads. | ☐ Social Hashtag Share a post using Monday's hashtag. |
| TUE | ☐ Get Personal Talk about a personal challenge or business idea with a mentor or expert. | ☐ Learning Day Educate yourself with 2 hours of YouTube videos. | ☐ Get Personal Talk about a personal challenge or business idea with an industry associate or expert. | ☐ Learning Day Educate yourself with 3 hours of YouTube videos or books. |

| WED | ☐ Promotion Day Share new content on your sales channels (an article, YouTube video, podcast) | ☐ Favorite Things Promote video content that your clients would love. | ☐ Promotion Day Share new content on your media channels. (an article, YouTube video, podcast) | ☐ Favorite Things Promote video content that your clients would love. |
|---|---|---|---|---|
| THUR | ☐ Inspire Others Share an inspiring thought or quote | ☐ Mail Day Send out at least 150 mailers to potential sellers. | ☐ Inspire Others Share an inspiring thought or quote. | ☐ Promote Your Brand Share one of your deals step by step. |
| FRI | ☐ Reflection Friday Share a milestone in your business. | ☐ Inquiry Day Encourage clients via live social media to throw in their questions and answer live. | ☐ Mail Day Send Out 150 Mailers to Potential leads. | ☐ Inquiry Day Encourage your clients via live social media to throw in their questions to answer live. |
| SAT | ☐ Feedback Day Ask for feedback on your services. | ☐ Consulting Day Share a simple industry hack. | ☐ Feedback Day Ask for feedback on your services. | ☐ Consulting Day Share a simple industry hack. |

Along with a calendar, using a real estate journal allows you to document your activities and decide what tasks are working better for you at what time, and what results you are getting.

You'll be amazed at how this journal will also help you in other aspects of your life. With a journal, you can see which marketing works for you (Meetup group, Real Estate Investors Club, seminar, etc.).

The journal and calendar will be the soul and heart of your diet. They will provide daily reminders of all the tasks in your plan. They will help you stay focused on your goals, and help you reassess your daily habits as needed.

Keep in mind that consistency, motivation, and effort will yield the results you are looking for on this diet. Make sure you do one thing a day towards your goal. Slow progress is still progress. An hour each day, five to six days a week, used efficiently, can help you attain your desired 90-day goal. Time efficiency and networking will be the keys to getting your desired result in 90 days or less. Anybody can dream it, but you'll never see it unless you are 100 percent committed to it.

You can start committing *now*. From here, I'll be including a section for you to write and gather notes at the end of each chapter. Begin practicing your diet prep plan by collecting your thoughts in the pages I've provided—trust me, it works.

> "*Time is simply how you live your life*" –Craig Sager

**Notes**

_____

_____

_____

_____

**Daily wins or accomplishments**

_____

_____

_____

_____

_____

_____

Documenting any accomplishments big or little is important to keep you on plan. Look forward to using your notes and charting your results. Write down your goals in the notes section, and as you complete the plan or reach a milestone, compare your wins and accomplishments to your notes.

## The Importance of Realistic Thinking and Taking Calculated Risk

In the beginning, you will be pumped up about the new plan, thinking you're going to close the first person you speak to about raising funds, or the first property you sourced that called you back. Realistically, that will not happen. In sales and marketing, we would use the law of averages. From what I discovered, the 10

Percent Rule seems even more accurate. Using this rule, if you market to 10 people, only one person is going to call you back. And the odds of you closing that deal are 50/50. Set expectations, but be realistic in your thinking about results.

When I started in real estate, we would send around a thousand postcards a month, only spoke with four people, and close one. That one was usually a wholesale deal because we didn't have the funds or the resources to acquire the deal, so it paid for marketing the next month as we continued to build and network. After six months or so, I was able to start joint venturing on deals.

People say investing in real estate is risky, but not investing in your financial future is even more risky. Statistically speaking, with the rise of inflation and the high likelihood of social security being bankrupt for most people when retirement hits, we can't afford not to take the risk and start the real estate investing diet.

I spoke in Chapter 2 about being an abundant thinker. People that have this way of thinking live in a non-negotiable way of thinking, meaning there is no lack, there is only more or there is a solution or there is a way. If they finally do get a call, but don't have the money available to purchase the deal 100 percent, being an abundant thinker means they would already know which exit strategy to use for the particular deal, whom to contact, or if they should walk away. Most people that start in real estate investing don't get a deal for two years, mainly because of the learning curve associated with trying to find deals, building the network, and what to do once a deal is found.

The key to making millions in real estate investing is to be in a state of resourcefulness constantly. Successful people are not all geniuses, or coming from trust funds. In all actuality, most people started from ground zero. The common denominator is their ability to be resourceful and think realistically.

> *"Risk comes from not knowing what you are doing"*
> *–Warren Buffet*

## Daily Intake

Like any diet, you have a daily caloric intake. If you're trying to gain weight, you take in more calories; if you are trying to lose weight, you must put your body in a caloric deficit. If you're trying to become a real estate investor and make millions of dollars, you have to have a daily intake of real estate investing education. You must spend, at minimum, an hour each day learning about the different aspects of real estate, particularly in the area where you wish to invest. For instance, if you're trying to gain weight and based on your weight, you must consume 2,200 calories a day, and you're consuming 1,000, what do you think is going to happen? What do you think the results will be if you're working out and only consuming 1,000 calories a day, and you're trying to gain weight? Nothing, you are defeating the purpose of one; being on a diet and number two, you will never get any results, and if you do, it would be the opposite of the results you are looking for.

Now that there's an understanding of the importance of your daily intake to achieve desired results, let's break down what you will need to do.

Start your day

Day is over:

Commute & Learn

5-7x a week for 90 days

Eat dinner

Eat Breakfast

Real Estate time

Wake up

- ➤ Wake up: Start by giving thanks for something great in your life, or think of something to be grateful for, i.e. waking up. *(Don't check text messages or emails, as it will dictate the next hour or the rest of your day.)*
- ➤ Eat a healthy breakfast: Your energy levels are in direct correlation with your productivity and success.
- ➤ Commute to work, school, or staying home: Listen to a real estate investing podcast or watch a video on YouTube about real estate investing.
- ➤ Start your day: Do you *(whatever that is).*
- ➤ Day is over: 9-5 or whatever you do to keep the lights on.
- ➤ Eat dinner: Something delicious.
- ➤ After dinner: One to two hours of real estate investing education, searching for deals, or marketing.
- ➤ Sleep: Figure out the amount of sleep your body needs to perform at a high level.

Repeat this three days per week for mediocre results. To

achieve optimal results, repeat five to seven days a week consistently for 90 days.

I know that some people reading this just made a thousand excuses in their head for why this is not possible. Most people give the excuse of time. However, people make time for the things they want to make time for. Let's think about this for a moment. There are 24 hours in a day. We have eight hours to sleep, eight hours for most people to work, four hours to eat and spend time with family. This leaves four hours to do...what? How important is your financial future? What is your "why" for wanting to be rich, financially independent, or your own boss?

**WHY?**

_____

_____

_____

_____

_____

_____

_____

## Marketing for Dollars

Now the exciting part: marketing for dollars. What you're about to learn now is the most exciting part of the money-making process, but also the most tedious. Over the next couple of pages, I'm going to give you different strategies that will be the key "ingredients" to this diet. The majority of these strategies have originated from real estate gurus, marketing consultants and advertising agencies, and take years and millions of dollars to learn. You'll learn different techniques for finding amazing deals and motivated sellers. These techniques are so easy that anyone can use them. You can complete these steps in one to two hours each day. If you want to see results on this diet, think of this as your exercise for the day.

From this point on, you will have a killer advantage over anyone just starting out in real estate who's not on this diet. What you're about to learn may seem unorthodox, but trust me when I tell you stick to the plan, and you will get results. These are the only techniques I used to acquire properties, even multi-family units—these techniques work for any type of real estate.

Once you get these processes automated, you will have an overflow of leads continuously every month. Just like on any diet, we will start with the simple no-cost or low-cost approach, but it will capture the attention of motivated sellers.

With that being said, getting leads starts by getting into the mindset that you're here to help people by taking the stress and pressure off the seller. Basically, you're here to help solve a problem. Don't think that you're taking advantage of a seller who is in a bad situation—that's counterproductive to the goal you and the seller are trying to accomplish. Keep in mind that these strategies will work in any market and any economic climate.

Advertising is a form of communication, and like with any relationship, what you say may be different from what that person interprets. Thus, the first thing you want to understand is who you're targeting. This will allow you to use different ways to advertise your message. After all, you can't use the same strategy or advertising message for all sellers, as people don't all respond to the same message in the same way.

## Headlines

No matter what type of outlet you use (flyers, bandit signs, email, classified ads on Craigslist, business cards, etc.), the communication that the person sees first is the headline. The average attention span is about eight seconds and has decreased over time due to technology and things like social media. The headline is very important, because this is what gets people to go straight to your ad over anything else and read the details of your offering.

Headlines should be big and bold, but not overbearing. Take, for instance, the examples below:

- ➢ Direct approach: "We buy ugly houses."
- ➢ Indirect approach: "Don't get stuck like he did."
- ➢ Question: "Do you need to sell your home in 7 days, all cash?"
- ➢ How: "Want to learn how to sell your home quick with no agent?"
- ➢ Authoritative or call to action: "Sell your home now! / Call us today!"

Testimonials also help for properties that are for sale by owners i.e., in cases of divorce, estate holders, and sometimes even sellers going into foreclosure and looking for a company they can trust. With any of these, be very specific in the headlines. People don't like equivocal language—again, the average attention span is too short, and they have probably seen dozens of flyers and ads.

When you're creating your advertising and marketing material, keep in mind that people who are motivated to sell their home are always interested in the fastest way to sell their homes and make money ASAP. A quick list of situations that fit this target includes:

- Facing foreclosure
- Work relocation
- Second-home owners
- Vacant owners
- Inheritance
- Estate sale
- Divorce
- Downsizing
- Job loss
- Medical bills

Your offering has to be compelling to the seller because, again, they may have had a lot of offers already. The more you can identify and address specific concerns of the people you advertise to, the higher the response rate you'll get from qualified sellers.

One of the key advantages is that neither you nor the seller really spend anything out of pocket if a transaction is never realized. You would be out of pocket the mailing cost, and maybe an earnest money deposit of a hundred bucks. In any of your marketing ads, emphasize there being no risk, no money out of pocket, and a short amount of time for them to achieve their desired results. Always remember that the people in the above list may not have had anyone reach out to offer a solution to their problem. They will more than likely will agree to a sale that can take place in 30 days or less.

## Direct Mail

Direct mail is the most cost-effective marketing strategy you can use. Flyers and postcards are very quick to make because so many are pre-made. They're also super cheap to print, and you can either put them in the mail when you're driving for dollars, or you can get leads by mailing them to a specific name and address. (Postcards and flyers are sometimes not as effective if you don't have the recipient's full name—in that case, they'll likely throw them in the trash.) Always keep in mind that your direct mail flyer or postcard still needs to convince the person of a call to action.

The name of your business, and the color of the flyer, are really irrelevant to the person you're mailing to. They are only interested in solving a problem, so your direct mail campaign has to be compelling enough for them to see if you can solve their problem.

Always remember that these are real people. They have real needs, so reverse the roles when you receive a call from a prospect. I learned in sales to let the client speak as much as possible, as this will allow you to use exactly what they are saying in your favor. They will provide you with the information, if you allow them to. Even though you might know the answer and end result because you've done this before or feel like your training is sufficient, speaking too much will not only hinder you from building rapport (the most important part of any deal), but it will also disengage the prospect. You can easily talk yourself out of a deal by being a know-it-all.

When I worked in banking, my clients would come in with a problem or a need, and I would sit at my desk and let them ramble on. Doing so allowed me to uncover countless opportunities I wouldn't have if I hadn't let my clients talk. I would ask open-ended questions genuinely to establish trust and rapport. By doing this, I was able to shatter my goals every quarter. For example, a client would come in and say, "I need to open an account because my daughter is leaving for college in two years. I want to put money aside for her once she graduates." To the average person, it seems like she just needs to open a savings account to put aside money. But I heard the need for a savings account *as well as* other opportunities, such as a possible checking and savings account for her daughter, and a money market savings account, depending on the amount she wants to put aside. It also allowed me to ask additional questions to uncover more opportunities, such as "Do you have any other kids graduating soon?" or "Any kids who may need a 529 plan?"

Have you ever had a conversation where you may have said five words, while the other person talks the majority of the time, but at the end of the conversation, that person seems energized and says, "That was a great conversation" or "You're really nice?" That's because people like to be heard, and great listeners are hard to find. Motivated sellers like to talk about their problems, and if you let them, the additional opportunities are endless. I can't express to you how many times we've had a motivated seller call in to sell us one property, and we end up finding out about their entire portfolio of homes, or an additional home they are about to sell, or a friend who's in real estate and needs someone to buy their home, as well. I tell anyone I mentor that if you want to get wealthy in real estate investing, shut up and listen.

To get started quickly, you can go to any flyer or postcard site, pick out stock images or premade templates, and add content like the examples below:

- Sell your house fast in 7 days without an agent Call 123-456-7899
- Facing foreclosure?? We can STOP IT. 123-456-7899
- Want to sell your property in 21 days, all cash? 123-456-7899
- AVOID the competition!! No agents, no fees, short sales, no waiting. 123-456-7899

It depends on the market if a local number or an 800 number matters to sellers or not. I recommend doing a variation of both for at least 60 days—within that time, you should have touched sellers a minimum of three times with direct mail, before you decide to move on to another lead list.

Keep in mind that if it's a foreclosure list, you may not want to get rid of it, because there is a very high likelihood that the people on that foreclosure list will end up on it again in the near future. I can recall several occasions where, a year later we would get calls from people whom we spoke previously that either didn't want our help or were able to do a "Band-Aid" fix.

If you're looking for leads, there are quite a few companies that you can Google to get leads of all kinds, from 60 to 90 days late, vacant homes, probate, etc. You name the situation, and there's a lead list out there. I will not name any specific companies for legality issues, as results vary for each individual.

If you don't have money to pay for leads, I'm going to provide you with a free tip that is worth the price of this book 1,000 times over, and you can use it from anywhere. If you never want to spend a dollar on leads, but want to achieve amazing results and find the best deals that are specific for you and your investing needs, use this tip. All you need is a computer or phone, an Excel spreadsheet, and at least one to two hours.

Here is the tip:

Go to Zillow.com and type in the zip code or address of the area and market of interest. Once you have pulled up the area, click on the filter that says "For Sale." The filter should drop down and give you the following options: "For Sale," "Potential Listings," "For Rent" and "Sold."

Uncheck all the boxes except for the one that says "Potential Listings." Leave that with the check in the box. Click on the drop-down that says "Potential Listings" and uncheck "Fore-closed." The only boxes that should have a check in them should be "Pre-Foreclosure" and "Make Me Move." These will be your motivated sellers.

Some of the Pre-Foreclosure listings will give you the auction date, the status of the property, and the last reported amount, which will give you an idea of how much equity is possibly in the home and what the bank is looking for from the seller. That amount is also the amount that the bank will possibly take if the home goes into foreclosure. If you see that the home has an auction date one or two months out, you know that the home-owner is either still in the home and is very motivated, or they have vacated the home (and it's still very motivated), or that they are living in the home and in denial that they're going to lose it.

These are the people that you should target first with your direct mail campaign. You may even be tempted to go door-knocking if it is a really good deal. As I mentioned before, it is always ideal to have the homeowner's name when sending out mailers and postcards, but for now, take the address and you put it on the Excel spreadsheet to save for your direct mail campaign. You may be able to use White Pages to type in the address and get a homeowner's name, or you can pay for a search on websites such as TruthFinder. You could always go to the county website, but don't spend too much time trying to find a homeowner's name. Focus on getting as many addresses as you can through this process and saving them to the Excel spreadsheet. I recommend putting down the date when you first mailed out to them, and also the date (if you can find one) of the auction. If the person contacts you from your mailing campaign, put that date down, as well.

Starting with this strategy will allow you the highest probability of achieving your desired goal in 90 days or less. It's free, and will only cost you the price of stamps, time, sweat equity, and if you choose to go door-knocking, gas money. I strongly recommend doing this over any other lead generation process, as it will give you by far the highest return on investment.

I know a few of you may be thinking, "What about apartments or commercial properties?" You can do something similar with the properties on LoopNet, but getting the current owner's address is a bit of a challenge, it's not as straightforward with knowing the status of the properties, and the turnaround time on the lead is not as fast. I would focus on using Zillow to close the deal on a motivated seller in 90 days or less.

## Classified Ads

I won't spend too much time on classified ads, as they don't yield results as fast as other strategies. Still, they are a good way to drive traffic to your website or 800 number.

You have quite a few options with free classifieds online, so just pick the one that makes sense for you. Some people use newspapers, but I found that to be outdated, considering the era in which we're in with technology. We would typically post seven to 10 different ads on Craigslist in each market of interest and just copy-paste the ad copy from Notepad which makes the process faster, and we got a pretty good amount of phone calls in specific markets. For instance, Los Angeles, California proved to be a useless market for these types of ads because within five minutes of refreshing the page, our ad was on page three because of the rapid pace of postings. Augusta, Georgia's classified ads worked well—we received a lot of calls and got great leads with the ad postings. It worked great in Orlando, Florida, as well. My advice is to try it in your market for 30 to 90 days and see if it's effective and worth the time spent.

Believe it or not, three five-line ads can drive amazing leads, so don't think it has to be extremely wordy. You just have to make sure your headline is bold, with a call to action, and know exactly who you're targeting and what type of leads you are trying to capture. A key thing to remember is the demographic. If you are in a highly-populated Latin Community, you may want to create ads in Spanish. To get the most response with your ads, try to use words like FREE and HELP, and even language like, "Aren't you ready to sell your home?" "Isn't it time to stop foreclosure?" "Haven't you tried everything?" A question added after a statement is designed to displace resistance, provoking the reader to do exactly what your call to action is requesting. You can also use statements such as, "Do you want to sell your home now or later?" or "Would you like to be stress free or debt free?" These offer the illusion of choice, but both choices are preferable and advantageous for you to get a potential lead.

A quick list of different ad headlines that yielded results for us:

- Facing foreclosure? Need help?
- Free home selling advice
- 7 Ways to sell your home in 14 days with no agent
- Need help?
- 7 secrets to sell your home fast with no money
- Call our 24-hour pre-recorded message for free foreclosure advice
- Call for your free foreclosure guide
- Need to sell your home fast behind on mortgage?
- Got foreclosure?

Those are the headlines we used to keep a constant flow of leads. Some of them were good, some of them were bad, and for the ones that didn't leave a message when they called in, we would just check the caller ID and call the number back to see what their need is. They obviously had a reason to call, so don't be afraid to cold-call numbers if they called you but didn't leave a message.

In the body of the ad, don't be too lengthy. Remember, people have a short attention span, especially if they're facing foreclosure. When anxiety is high, it's appropriate to keep it as simple as possible.

For any type of marketing, I suggest getting an additional phone line or even the 800 number that has a recorded message. This will help you screen for motivated sellers and people that need your help. I would advise using a 24-hour pre-recorded message or something of that nature or even your personal phone if you're comfortable with random people calling you

Marketing and advertising are the lifeblood of your business. You have to constantly be advertising, as that's how you will get deals. Have faith that what you're doing is going to yield results. Starting out, you may send a thousand postcards and never get a phone call, or you may post on Craigslist 10 times a week and feel like it's not working. Like anything, tweak and make pivots when you find out what works. Keep your mind in the mental state dad marketing and advertising is a key to your success in real estate investing or any business.

What I want you to do now is make a list of all the places where you want to place ads, the type of ads, and which you will start with. Just like any diet, you must prep for the week if you want to make sure you don't slip up. Make a plan for yourself at the beginning of every week.

# Marketing and Advertising Plan

| Objective (Insert your marketing objective, one per line) | Target Audience (Who your marketing objective aims at) | Action (Every promo- tional action that will accom- plish your objective) | Timescale (The time allowed for each process or advertis- ing plan) | Investment (Amount and time spent on marketing steps) | Result Metrics (Measure of success of each action) |
|---|---|---|---|---|---|
| | | | | | |
| | | | | | |
| | | | | | |
| | | | | | |

CHAPTER 4

# ACQUIRING AND EXIT STRATEGIES

IN ANY BUSINESS, YOU need cash flow, capital gains, and ancillary income. With real estate, you can do all three without ever using your own money. I increased my net worth to $1 million in right around seven months using other people's money (OPM) and only investing in real estate.

I was interested in real estate, but my approach was wrong. I kept trying to do everything on my own, using my own money to buy everything. I tried to build investing dollars through doing options, buying stock outright, and even trying to get in on IPOs, but nothing was building my nest egg quick enough for me to purchase real estate. If you lost money in the stock market, don't feel bad—that's part of the journey in becoming wealthy.

At the time when I started, I had about $23,000 in credit card debt because I was trying to build my app InvestFar with the money that I had when I was working in banking and trading stock. I took all of the excess money I had and dumped it in the market to generate more income. It worked temporarily, but it still wasn't giving me enough income to purchase investment properties and get out of the rat race. While working at the bank, I discovered the strategies that I'm about to outline in this chapter. Not only can you purchase investment properties with these OPM techniques, but you can also purchase your dream home the same way, and actually even have the seller pay you to buy their home.

Imagine what it would be like to have someone pay you to buy your dream home from them. Stop thinking about getting up and going to a job you hate, or worrying about how to pay the bills next month. Imagine being able to go to the store and buy whatever you want without looking at the price tag.

## A Word About Fix-And-Flip

By the end of this section, you'll realize that "fixing and flipping" is not the only way to be a real estate investor. It is, in fact, the most expensive and least efficient way to start out investing in real estate.

I advise against it, but I know many of you will still go out and do fix-and-flips, just as I did when my mentor told me not to. It's interesting that when you tell a person not to do something, they do the exact opposite sometimes, because they think they can do it better than you, or that the same thing won't happen to them. Experience is the best teacher—just don't say I didn't warn you.

There are better and easier ways to get into real estate investing that don't require you to monitor bad contractors, go over budget, or stall your flip for weeks because you ran out of money. If you decide to fix and flip, you will 100 percent run into at least one of these issues. If you do flips long enough, you will encounter all three, unless you know something that all the other active real estate investors don't.

I'm not discouraging you from the fix-and-flip because I think there's profit in it, but I would advise you to do something different if you're starting out, until you build enough working cash flow and have deep pockets. I still don't like the idea of fix-and-flipping because there is no cash flow coming from the property. If you took out hard money to purchase the home, you're paying a mortgage note out of your free cash flow every month, because there's no tenant in the house while you're flipping it.

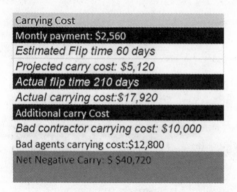

Carrying Cost
Montly payment: $2,560
Estimated Flip time 60 days
Projected carry cost: $5,120
Actual flip time 210 days
Actual carrying cost:$17,920
Additional carry Cost
Bad contractor carrying cost: $10,000
Bad agents carrying cost:$12,800
Net Negative Carry: $ $40,720

For instance, I had a luxury home in Las Vegas, Nevada that I flipped because it was an amazing deal. However, the mortgage was $2,560 a month, and there was no tenant in the property. The house was initially supposed to be flipped in 60 days, but the contractor decided to walk off the job and made off with $10,000. Me and the agent had to spend a few weeks looking for a replacement contractor, which added more time. The flip went from two months to seven months, which cost us $17,920 ($2,560 times seven) in just holding cost on the "fix and flip." On top of that, it took an additional 5 months to sell the property because of the initial agent we used and the timing of the market. This tacked on another $12,800 in holding cost. All told, it was $30,720 down the drain, and we exited the deal with not as much profit as we'd have liked. The headache on "fix and flips" is not worth it in the beginning. Unless you are starting out in multifamily unit "fix and flips"—that changes the narrative, especially if it's 50 to 75 percent occupied, because you would have cash flow coming in to help with debt coverage.

Again, I don't disagree with fix-and-flips, but I strongly recommend starting out instead with some of the strategies I'm going to get into now.

## The OPC Approach

There are only a few ways to buy real estate: your cash or credit, or other people's cash or credit. The average person doesn't have millions of dollars (or even thousands) sitting around in an account. In fact, most people live paycheck to paycheck, which means just over broke. So would it be smart to risk losing all of your money? Or would it be better to use other people's money? You can even use a hard money lender, but you'll still be required to put at least 10 percent down, so you're still out of pocket something.

In the beginning when I started investing in real estate, I used hard money or private lenders and the 10 percent I borrowed from an investor. I did this because the deals that I selected had enough equity for me to support giving away 10 percent on the borrowed funds for the down payment of the loan. That's another way I was able to generate wealth pretty quickly: finding great deals with a lot equity. Even though the properties had a lot of equity, it was still considered very risky, as the lender is funding up to 90 percent of the loan, and like most banks, hard money lenders also require a personal guarantee, so I was technically using my credit if anything were to go wrong in the deal. Even though I did it under a business name, they will still be able to go after me, because you have to offer a personal guarantee, even when you're operating as a business.

I'm not against hard money lenders. I still use them to this day. But there are still better methods to acquire deals that don't require hard money. Sometimes interest rates are favorable, depending on the value of the property. You just have to find the right lender for your credit criteria, and one that's right for this specific deal.

For a few deals, I've also used private money. It was very easy to do because of the type of deals that I brought to the table, but I had established relationships with the people that I was getting private money from. You have to have a great track record with the people that you're looking to get private money from. This is always a great option, but it's very hard to do starting out, because you have to have that trust there. If you've never flipped a home or know little about real estate, getting private money from someone other than your parents or a family member will be almost impossible. This goes back to networking—going to real estate investment clubs, and becoming friends with other investors because meeting investors in these types of environments, they tend to be more understanding about the position that you're in and may be more willing to loan you a personal loan because they've been in your shoes before

But again, this can be tricky in the beginning, and if you're trying to reach your desired results in 90 days or less, this may not be feasible for you. A hard money loan could be the route you could go, depending on your credit, but there is a better way then hard money or private lenders. Other people's credit (OPC) requires you to do nothing but the steps outlined in your daily diet plan.

OPC is the safest and most self-protective way to invest in real estate when starting out. It requires little capital and mainly sweat equity. If you're looking to reach your desired results in 90 days or less, this is the quickest, least expensive and safest way to reach your goal. This method works in any economic climate—in a downturn, a recession, or even when the economy is hot. People get divorced, die, lose their jobs, or need to relocate for work in any economic state.

There are a few advantages benefits of OPC:

> You don't need 10 percent down.
> You don't have to qualify for credit.
> There is no risk to you or your business.
> You will never run out of deals.

## How OPC Works

I'm sure the thought in your mind right now is about how to use other people's credit on a mortgage or to buy a house. It is actually pretty simple to grasp.

The key is leaving the loan in place for the existing mortgage by getting the deed. When a title company or closing attorney prepares the sale or purchase of a home, in a typical closing, the deed is notarized and recorded at the county recorder's office by the owner. The person who took out the mortgage to buy the property is now the owner of that home, but they borrowed the money from the lender to purchase that home. The deed is in the owner's name, but the bank has a lien on the title, and can take over the property if the owner defaults on paying the loan. So all you have to do is get the deed!

Once the deed lists your name (or your company name) as a grantee, you will be the owner of that home. The seller would still be responsible for the existing loan, not the new owner. It doesn't matter how you took ownership of the home—you could have paid $10 to get the deed, or they could have paid you $5,000 to take the deed. None of it matters with respect to ownership. It's your home once your name is signed on the deed, that's all that matters. You now have full control of that property. Even if the seller decides to change their mind after the deal has been done, once the deed has been signed there's nothing they can do, not even in court.

This is how you use other people's credit. You really don't need to understand how all of this works, because once you go to a closing attorney or title company, they will do it all for you at closing. The process works like any typical purchase-and-sale agreement. It's a regular closing, but the fees are different, depending on how you structure the deal.

## Why OPC Works

I know the next thought in your mind is, "Why would someone sign over the deed to their home?"

This is where having credibility plays a huge part: getting a person in a distressed situation to trust you requires as host of different things but credibility is the main part in convincing someone to give up their most expensive asset. If you don't make payments after you sign the deed, the seller will get in trouble and the payments will be reported on their credit report, because they are the ones who originated the loan so regardless of who owns the deed, they are still responsible for the monthly payment until the debt is paid off. They personally guaranteed the loan, not the home. Never make a promise to a seller if you know you're not going to make payments. If you structure the deal to where you are going to sell the home in 30 days or less and you're not going to make payments, let that be known up front, so the seller knows what to expect and can agree to that type of sale, even though it has some form of risk for them.

Let's say, for example, that you have a seller going into foreclosure. They really have nothing to lose at this point—their credit is probably already ruined, and if they don't agree to a sale, they may never be able to purchase a home for the next two to five years. In a case like this, getting the deed is much harder, especially if the house is going to auction within a certain number of days or weeks.

Say, for instance, you sent out some postcards and made a couple cold calls, and you get a seller that's in foreclosure. You visit the seller and explain that you are going to purchase their home subject to the existing loan, because you would be able to sell the house in 14 days or in a shorter amount of time than a traditional real estate sale, which takes 30 to 45 days, depending on the lender. If a person is going to lose their home in seven days at an auction, they don't have 30 to 45 days to wait for a traditional sale. They'd be more inclined to sign over their deed to prevent foreclosure on their home. You have to offer them some money to move out sometimes or, depending on the situation, you may be able to have them give you money purchase their home. We had a scenario where the seller had two days left before his home was going to auction, and we were able to structure a deal where he paid all closing costs and two months of mortgage payments, so we could take over the property, do minor fixes like carpet and paint, and put it back on the market. The seller didn't have enough money to get the home market-ready, keep making payments, and catch up the arrears on the house; he was willing to cover closing costs and pay the monthly mortgage because he owed $7,300 in back payments and didn't want a foreclosure on his record. In this case, we put up a total of $14,750 to have the deed signed over to us to take control of the property, do a little bit of TLC, and get it listed on the market. In 45 days, we sold it, paid off his remaining balance to the bank, and made a net profit of $33,502.

Some people may think this is taking advantage of homeowners in a bad situation; that is the wrong mindset to have. We solved a problem and saved a person from a long-term issue by saving his credit and paying off his existing loan on a home that otherwise would have gone into foreclosure. It was a win for all parties involved.

You can also use this method to buy your dream home. People in all price ranges have struggles in life; we've found homeowners in million-dollar communities that were facing foreclosure, or just went through a divorce and no longer wanted the house. This strategy is not limited to only foreclosure; this process applies to the list I mentioned previously. Everyone has different motivations.

Subject to the existing loan, OPC (other people's credit) is the best way to achieve the desired results in 90 days or less. Understand this strategy is the best way to bypass borrowing money from a lender and using your own personal credit to accelerate yourself into financial independence or making you wealthy with real estate.

## Understanding the "Subject-To"

With subject-to the existing loan transactions, most of the time the seller does not get any proceeds from the sale, unless that was structured in the deal between you. What's most advantageous for them is relief from the situation, and no longer having to make payments. Many times, the only thing that is needed is closing costs, and if you pick the right title company or closing agent, those fees can be minimal. With this strategy, you will have acquired a home without ever talking to a bank, a hard money lender or a private lender, along with assuming no risk or liabilities. You can build a net worth of a million-plus without having any liabilities, which is the key to getting wealthy.

When you can identify what a seller's problem is, i.e., their pain point, they will sign over the deed. Think about when you're sick—all you want to do is take some kind of action to relieve the pain. There's no greater need than to relieve pain if someone's hurting. In order to do this, as I mentioned, you have to make sure that you build rapport and do the things that I have outlined in the previous chapter to get to this point.

In some cases, you can take one phone call, but in a majority of cases, you will do a lot of follow-up with the client. Most of them are in denial about their problem, so the key to getting a home subject-to is follow up, like with any sale. The more you follow up, the more the person will establish rapport with you. By the end of the cycle, you will more than likely have talked to the person three to five times, and quite a few hours.

Now I'm pretty sure you're thinking, "If this was so easy why doesn't everyone do it?"

That answer is simple: most people have never even heard of a subject-to. In fact, some title companies or closing attorneys have never even seen a deal like this. It is very important to educate yourself so that you can explain it to an attorney or title company when it's time for closing. It took me about two years to figure out this process. Even with having a mentor, there's a learning curve associated with learning how to do subject-to's. In conjunction with subject-to's, it's important to learn how to do short sales because in the event you get a distressed property owner who's willing to do a subject-to, it could be pending a foreclosure that needs to be stopped and submitting the property for a short sale with the bank is the way to do that.

With the ingredients in the book that I've given you, any of you can do this. The key ingredient you need is a seller who's even slightly motivated, and you can find those sellers in any market. Once you do your first subject-to, it'll be hard to focus on any other type of real estate investing in the single-family market.

I know many of you will make excuses like "All this is too hard" or "That doesn't work here" or "I can't do this because I don't know about contracts." Don't make excuses for yourself. You are the only obstacle to success. If you want to be successful doing this type of real estate investing, or any type of investing, you will find a way.

If your goal on this diet is to quit your job in 90 days or less, this process is the way to go.

## Exit Strategies

A lot of people make the mistake of acquiring a property before they think about how they're going to exit. When you find a property, before you get it under contract, you should first think about how you're going to exit the property. This will determine how you are going to make a profit, and also help you choose the best option to give you the highest return. Depending on the property and your financial situation, the exit strategy will be different, so don't get a property under contract until you have thought of at least three exit strategies. Ultimately, you don't want to waste your time and the seller's time, especially if it's a home going into foreclosure. Every investor loves a great deal, so if you can come up with a strategy to make money along with an investor making money, it's a win-win for all three parties involved.

Based on the different ways you've learned to acquire properties, it will be easy for you to find buyers, because you will supply properties with more equity and they will be cheaper for the investor to acquire in most cases. Even in some cases that I'm about to explain, you may get some buyers who had bad credit, or can't get money from a financial institution due to a previous foreclosure, or they're just not qualified to purchase a home though they have the cash available. Some people can't afford the traditional down payments to purchase a home, but that doesn't mean they are high-risk tenants. Whatever the scenario may be, whether it's an investor or a home buyer who can't buy a home in the traditional way, these are often motivated and trustworthy people. The financial industry has changed the regulations, which has prevented a huge portion of the market from being able to purchase a home. Banks are a lot tighter on mortgage loan approvals, and it's a more strenuous process for them to lend due to the housing crisis in 2008. This has created an amazing opportunity for real estate investors with a skill set to acquire below-market investment properties to sell homes quickly.

Financing strategies from the past will not work in this economic climate, but what you learned in previous chapters will always work, now or in the future, because the list of motivated sellers that I provided will always be around.

## One Scenario, Three Strategies

I'm going to give you a scenario of a home we bought, along with three different exit strategies, and show you the profit you can make from it, depending on your own situation.

We had an absentee owner who lived in Maryland. His second home was in Georgia. The seller had to relocate for work and decided to keep the home. He left his son in the property, but after a few years his son decided he didn't want to live there anymore. The house was owned free and clear; the seller had no mortgage. It was in a great neighborhood, right next to the Augusta National Golf Course, where the Masters Tournament is played. The home's as-is value was $105,000. With cold calling and using mailers, we were able to get in touch with the seller. He was actually not in the market to sell but was not opposed to it; his son was tired of caring for the home, and the owners had no interest in keeping the property anymore. Through establishing a rapport with the seller by having several engaging conversations, we were able to put an offer in for $55,000. He stated that he was offered $60,000 for the property at one time. In the end, we settled on $57,500, and signed a purchase-and-sale agreement.

This home needed a little work, and at the time, we had three flips going and didn't want to take on another flip. But before we got the house under contract, we figured out our exit strategy.

*Wholesaling is getting a property under contract which is the purchase and sale agreement and then selling (assign) that contract to a buyer with a premium attached which is your fee in addition to the seller's price for that contract.*

At first, we thought about wholesaling the property for $67,000. We would make a $10,000 profit by doing no work except for speaking with the seller and marketing. The after-repair value (ARV) for the home was around $132,000. Based on the repair estimate we did, which came out to around $35,500, that would leave a great profit of $29,500 to an investor. The flip would take about 45 days, as the home was in good shape; they could do even less rehab and turn a higher profit.

| Fix and Flip Deal Flow |
| --- |
| Hard Money Debt @9% |
| Purchase price: $45,000 |
| Included Rehab budget: $35,500 |
| Pay myself: $19,000 |
| Total Loan amount: $99,500 |
| Property Sold: $130,000 |
| Net Profit: $49,500 |
| Paid upfront: $19,000 |
| Paid at sale: $30,500 |

*Do the flip the right way, or you will be stuck in a home that no one wants to purchase since it wasn't completed correctly. Always remember that you get what you pay for, and you will pay for bad quality in the end. Trust me, I know!*

Once we ran through that scenario and saw the return we could make flipping the home, we made the decision to flip the property, as we also needed the cash flow. I know you're thinking, "How do you make cash flow before the flip is done?" This is where knowing all facets of creative financing works. I had a line of credit to purchase homes, which the lender provides 100 percent rehab and 90 percent on the purchase price. We knew the seller was motivated and needed the money, so we called him back and asked him to sell us the home for $45,000, to close in seven days. He agreed. I took out a loan for $64,000 to purchase the home, paying myself $19,000 up front, while the seller would get his $45,000. The bank funded 100 percent of the $35,500 rehab, for a total loan of $99,500, and we sold the home for $130,000, making an additional $30,500 profit with no money out of pocket. We gave an investor 12 percent interest on the 10 percent down payment for the hard money loan.

I advised earlier not to do fix-and-flips or hard money loans. But in scenarios like this, when you run through all the exit strategies, you can see where using a hard money lender to do a fix-and-flip makes sense. When you are starting out, and if you are trying to reach your 90-day goal, I would advise on wholesaling in a scenario like this. Some people may think of raising the fee for the contract. (I think when you get deals like this it's important not to be greedy and lose the deal completely.) Flip the contract, take the profits, and repeat the same process of wholesaling, and you can see that in 90 days or less, you can reach your goal. Wholesale five contracts at $10,000 each, and you have $50,000 in the bank with minimal work. Do five at $5,000, and you have $25,000. Do the math on what works for you in your market to reach your goal.

Another exit strategy that I didn't mention is a lease option. This would be something you could do later, after you have free cash flow available or a nice savings.

*Lease option is a property owner and a tenant agree at the end of the rental term period of the said property, the renter has the option of purchasing the property.*

In certain scenarios, when you have a motivated seller and you take a property subject to the existing loan or take control of the home, as I mentioned in previous chapters, you get the deed which gives you control of the property. You can then fix the property up a little, if needed, and rent it out to a potential buyer who can't afford the home in a traditional way. You would take a deposit up front of $10,000 (or whatever you decide) and lease that property to the tenant for the specified term. Once the term is up and the renter wants to buy the home, you will apply that $10,000 deposit to the down payment of the home. Should the tenant decide to move out and not buy the home, you get to keep the $10,000 deposit.

This scenario works great later in your real estate investment career. As you start to build a portfolio, the name of the game is cash flow, and this is one of the best ways to do it if you want to be in the single-family investment market.

There are many other ways to exit properties, but these are the main ways to generate the wealth you are seeking in the shortest amount of time in the single-family market. These same principles apply in multi-family and commercial markets but have a much longer turnaround time.

## Start Out Simple

On this particular diet, and to achieve the desired goal in the shortest amount of time, your only focus for the next 90 days is to do marketing, get homes under contract, and assign the contract to a buyer for a fee. Wholesaling is the only exit strategy you should be doing for the next 60 to 120 days.

My hope is that you apply this diet starting today. Most people say, "I'm going to start my diet on Monday" when it's Tuesday, or they say, "I'm going to start tomorrow," which never comes because there's always tomorrow.

For some, this will be just another diet plan that they half-ass and don't get results from, and then complain that it doesn't work. For many, this may be just another book they read. Ultimately, with any diet, the results will be temporary until you make that diet a lifestyle. Nobody walks around lean and in shape all year on a diet. It's a lifestyle, and you will have to stick to the same techniques that got you the results that you wanted, in order to maintain those results.

The key is to stay consistent. Generally, diets have an expiration date, unless while on the diet you find something in particular you like about it or see results. Then you're going to stay consistent with it; it then becomes your lifestyle.

Make this diet a lifestyle. You now have a plan that will change your life, so that you can live a lifestyle that you deserve. I want you to be successful just as I am. Take action now!

**Notes**

_____

_____

_____

_____


**Daily wins or accomplishments**

_____

_____

_____

_____

_____

_____

_____

CHAPTER 5

# WHAT NOW?

ACTION IS WHAT COMES now. This is the part that the majority of people who go to seminars or buy investing and business programs have a hard time with. Statistically, only 3 percent of people that go to seminars take action once they leave. People spend thousands of dollars going to seminars over and over again, then complain about it not working. A lot of people become seminar junkies and spend more money than they actually have when they attend buying programs. I know quite a few people who have maxed out credit cards to buy programs, do the courses, and never yield any fruit. It's not because the programs are bad. It's because they don't take action when it's completed. You can go to hundreds of seminars and even learn from them, but without action, it's impossible to get results.

People always quote **"Knowledge is power."** But it should be,

"*Knowledge is power if used.*" Just knowing something doesn't give you power. Think about all the things you have knowledge of. What kind of power has that given you, if you're sitting on your couch watching TV?

You should take action with this diet plan as though you need it to survive. *When your will to be successful is as strong as your will to stay alive, you will be successful.* Think about that. If you were in a situation where you were possibly going to die, but you had reasons on WHY you want or need to stay alive, what would you do? Human nature instinctively puts your mind and body into survival mode, which puts your brain in direct mode, allowing you to think of ways to stay alive. That is the type of mode you need to be in constantly, so that you take action and achieve the desired results. Most successful people were in that state of mind until they reached their goal; then, and only then, were they able to occasionally go on default mode. I don't suggest anyone on this diet to go on default mode unless or until they reach a point of having multiple income streams. The average millionaire has seven income streams. I'd actually advise once you have made this diet a lifestyle that you read *Multiple Streams of Income* by Robert G Allen; it will give you a lot of insight on when it's a good idea to take your foot off the gas and go on autopilot.

## Successful Execution

I provided you with a seven-day calendar in Chapter 3 that you should duplicate and make at least 90 days, if not longer. This is meant to make your list of actions simple and easy to start, but to also help you quantify what you are doing and keep track of what's working or not.

Another important thing *not* to do now is worry about creating an LLC, getting incorporated, or any of that. It's not important at this point. Why spend money on getting incorporated when you don't have a deal? Those funds should go toward marketing. Is it smart to start your real estate investing career in the red over an LLC? Take action, follow the diet, close on your first deal, and then if you really want to incorporate after that deal, you won't be using your own income—it would be investment income. Get a deal first!

That said, here is what will set you up for success at the execution phase. Whether you are a newbie or have a few years of experience in the industry, but are yet to get to the goals you envision for yourself, then you must start.

Before delving into the main "juice" of this section, I would like to make a one thing clear.

Getting started can be overwhelming. A lot of time can be spent on books, seminars and courses to know the drill but to also familiarize yourself with real estate investing. Increasing your education on the subject matter is not always the solution you need, at least at this point.

The more knowledge you acquire, the more your awareness increases, and the choices and challenges associated with different types of real estate transactions become wide open. As ironic as it seems, "analysis paralysis" is often the result of knowing too much. Knowledge is not bad, but it would be pointless if you are not moving forward with your acquired knowledge.

The following are nine actionable steps that will drive your real estate dream to become a reality. For absolute results, you just have to go through each step, educate yourself thoroughly, do proper property due diligence and then make practical decisions before doing your real estate deals. Only then can you reap the full rewards of moving through the real estate plan, whether you are a newbie, or you have spent years toiling to find your feet in the industry.

## 1. Know Your Financial Stage

You are to view real estate investing as a financial improvement driver. Before delving into any aspect of real estate, you must be aware of your entire financial profile.

New real estate investors have a common goal of attaining financial independence. You should view this as the mountain peak, where all your investments cover every bit of your living expenses.

The principle behind scaling this mountain applies equally to either real estate or any other business niche. To reach this point in a shorter time, your saving rate must increase. Your savings now form the basis of the investment, which can be used for any preferred asset such as real estate.

Identifying your position on the financial stage will help determine your next line of action. Are you at the bottom? Then you must seek out financing through hard money lending, raising funds or maybe even crowd funding for funds to invest to get started. If you're on top, you are a step closer to investing. Depending on your financial stage, certain real estate investing strategies would be more relevant than others.

Take the first step to start investing in real estate, that's as simple as looking at what financial resources you have available to you, it's very important to know where you are on the financial stage when you're starting out so you know how to strategize. This process may be an eye opener and your account balances may not be perfect, but it has to be done.

## 2. Choose an Investing Strategy

There are several strategies floating about for real estate investing. You may be tempted to create a 50-page business plan that will wow anyone who comes across it. Just bear in mind that starting the process is the most important thing. Look for something simple; the bigger, bulkier stuff can come up at a much later time. That is, if you still want it.

At this point, choose any applicable real estate investing strategy that will improve your financial stage. Selecting one strategy does not mean you are stuck with it until the end of time. You can decide to change directions a bit, or completely, at a later time. For now, your strategy just gives you the platform to begin. Also know that life happens, and to make the most out of it, you must be very flexible. Starting with one strategy will build focus and give you the needed confidence to pull off your real estate investing journey. Here are some strategies to help you move into stability.

➤ Survival Strategy

Goal: Increase your income, learn, and cut costs.

➤ Maintain your day job and work towards a raise.
➤ Rather than renting a home or stretching to make a home purchase, master-lease a residential property and rent all the units or bedrooms to reduce what you have to pay.

- Do a bit of bird-dogging for other investors in real estate. Sniff out amazing deals for them and learn how the investment acquisition process works.
- Be a buyer's agent. This involves helping buyers find properties and learn the process of retail there.
- Be a leasing agent. Learn the procedure of the landlord business by helping landlords match tenants with their properties.
- Help other investors supervise or manage their remodeling projects and learn how the remodeling business works from there.

Note that you can draft any option from the Survival strategy and combine with the following suggestions.

- Saver Strategy

Goal: Increase income and reduce expenses to drastically increase savings.

- Carry out some mortgage paydown principles to reduce your housing payment.
- To build large tax-free savings, flip your residence.
- Rent an accommodation, stay in it for a year or two, then rent it out.
- Begin wholesaling for smaller, quicker cash. This often requires money and time investment in marketing.
- Begin a side hustle away from real estate that matches your passion and skills with market demand. This will fetch extra cash for your growing income.

➢ Growth Strategy

Goal: Scale your small net worth into something bigger.

➢ Generate a large chunk of cash by fixing and flipping houses. Ensure you are saving, and reinvest the profits made.
➢ Build and grow a portfolio for income property with any of these plans:

- Trade-Up Plan: Build a strong income and equity portfolio using 1031 tax-free exchanges.
- Debt Snowball Plan: Buy a few properties and hasten up the debt paydown. Do this in bits, one property at a particular time.
- Self-Directed IRA: Tax-free investments in private loans, flips, or rentals using a 401k account or self-directed IRA.
- All-Cash Plan: Avoid debts and make 100 percent cash payment on every property.
- "Buy Three, Sell Two, Keep One" Plan: Purchase three rentals and hold on to them. Sell two, and repay the debt on the final one.

➢ Income Strategy

Goal: Increase income with less risk and hassle by turning equity into investments.

➢ Without Portfolio or Insufficient Properties

- Purchase limited partnership shares, commercial net-release rentals, high-quality residential rentals, and more passive assets.

  ➤ With Real Estate Portfolio

    - Increase income, reduce entire debt levels, and reduce risks by paying off debts.
    - Refinance any non-optimal debts remaining with low-interest and fixed long-term debts.
    - Sell properties of lower quality and use better ones to replace them.

  ➤ Diversify into other classes of assets.
  ➤ Make loans with funds inside or outside self-directed retirement accounts to other investors.

## Selecting a Strategy

On looking at the strategies above, you are likely to be interested in one or the other. Even though executing that strategy may seem intimidating at this point, all you have to do is note it down. There is still time for you to learn. The fascinating aspect of this part of the process is that it helps you identify the knowledge gaps you are lacking. Right now, pick a strategy that appeals to you, and move ahead to the next steps.

## 3. Select a Target Market

The market you decide on goes a long way in determining the

outlook of your results. Prices are high in a lot of locations, and you will have to decide whether to select a new market or make your investments close to home.

Investing close to home has a number of advantages. One advantage is that being a local gives you advanced knowledge of the market. This can translate into many things. You are likely to get firsthand information about the recent availability of higher-quality properties, or even have a deep connection with the history of the area. This is valuable in building trust with clients and endears your services to others.

I would prefer starting close to home, even though picking a market from a distance is still possible. If the prices in your locality are too high, you can explore other ideas to make the most of the market before looking elsewhere. Get into the suburb of the area, at least an hour's drive away from the city. These areas are increasingly affordable for investments and reasonable too. Another thing to do is identify smaller niches within the overall market of your choosing. Mobile homes, condos, and tax liens can be sometimes profitable in high-priced markets.

Regardless of where you select as a target market, close or afar, ensure that the first thing you do is a market analysis. Here is a brief highlight of what your market analysis will cover:

- ➢ Evaluation of location criteria (large scale)
- ➢ Population growth
- ➢ Jobs and economics
- ➢ Rent-to-price ratio
- ➢ Evaluation of location criteria (small scale)
- ➢ Barriers to supply
- ➢ Walkability

- Convenience
- Public transportation
- Infrastructure, local laws, finances, and taxes
- Crime rates and safety
- School districts

Selecting a target investment market gets easier by combining these criteria. The process of picking a target market really begins with a larger region, the metropolitan statistical area. To search for properties in easier ways, I advise narrowing this down to census blocks, zip codes or school districts.

If more time is needed in evaluating and choosing a market, it is still great—you are not off track. Still, do not dwell too long on it. I recommend that you make a choice as quickly as possible and move on to the next step. Making your way to actualize more financial freedom from real estate investing is not a perfect ride. You can test a hypothesis and backtrack your steps if it does not work.

## 4. Decide a Criteria

The criteria for your investment property will project what having a good investment is, both to you and to onlookers. Creating a written investment profile is often recommended, as it can be shared with investors, potential partners, and lead sources such as the real estate agents.

Here is what your investment profile should describe:

- Target property
- Ideal terms

After choosing a target market and an investing strategy you will be able to identify your target property with much ease. A target market is the focus of a particular group on a small segment within the overall market. You can adapt your investing strategy to whatever suits you.

The ideal terms help you determine your buying criteria, i.e., the amount you are willing to spend, type of property, rehab budget and max purchase price. This part of your investment profile largely depends on all the choices you have made until this point.

It is normal for you to change your criteria with time—as most investors do as their cash balances increase over time. Still, you have to make a decision to get started. Pick up something that you can make do with, at this point in time. Move forward to the next step toward realizing your goal of real estate investing. If there is a need to adjust your criteria along the way, you can easily make your way back and get the needed tweak done.

## 5. Team Building

If you are looking for a one-man sport, then you are not set for real estate. This is a team sport and you must take it for what it is. It is not a must that you have employees; still, you lead your team from the day you make the move.

Every advisor and independent contractor who offers support in one form or another is part of your team. If you are not interested in running this sort of team, then you might have to look to some other form of investing that suits you. Here are some of the most important people to make up your team.

- ➢ Inner Circle –These are your closest team members. They contribute to the collective cause on a personal level. Your spouse, personal advisers, mentors, and business partners are all part of this team
- ➢ Support Circle –You share a critical relationship with these people. They help in carrying out important and ongoing tasks. Your support circle might include property managers, real estate attorneys, certified public accountants, and lenders.
- ➢ Service Circle – Your service circle takes charge of the tasks needed in real estate investing. These personnel include the home inspector, plumber, electrician, handyman, closing agent, yard service, general contractor (when there is a need for major remodeling work), pest and moisture control, painter, etc.

You should note that you stand a better chance to find the core members of your team via networking with other investors in real estate.

Now that you have identified your team, you must move to the actionable step of the investing process.

## 6. Financing

Using financial facilities to make purchases in real estate is a common practice, unlike some other forms of investing. The good thing is that you have so many options to pick from, and can make use of any that suit your needs.

- ➢ Seller Financing – This form of financing is loved by a

number of people. A seller having equity gives you the room to make purchases by installments, or with the use of leases and other forms of creative contracts. Seller financing is not easy to access when compared to making a stroll into a bank, but its flexibility term makes it worth it.

➤ Portfolio Loans – With varying terms, portfolio loans are financial facilities kept by lending institutions or banks and are not sold in the mortgage market. They have competitive interest rates and a short-term ranging between five to 10 years.

➤ Veterans Administration Loans – To qualify for this, you must be a veteran, as the name implies. It is a long-term loan with a fixed interest rate and requires no down payment.

➤ Federal Housing Administration (FHA) Loans – This is a very easy loan to access, as it is insured by the federal government. It requires a down payment of little proportion, it is long-term, and has a fixed interest rate.

➤ Private Lenders – From wealthy individuals and money partners lending their money out, to self-directed IRAs and 401ks, private lenders vary widely. The long-term relationship and flexibility offered by private lenders make them valuable to any financing process.

➤ Conforming Loans – These loans conform to the guidelines of mortgage giants like Fannie Mae and Freddie Mac. The terms often include a fixed interest, long-term loan with five to 20 percent down payment.

➤ Hard Money Loans – Think of collateral and hard money loans. Here, the lenders are specific about the collateral involved (hard assets). Unlike other sources of financing where the detailed lending term is of priority, the costs of these loans are much higher and are often received for short-term projects.

You must bear in mind that selecting a financing method that suits you largely depends on the first line of action—that is, your financial situation. But it does not end here, as your strategy in Step 2 plays a role in your decision-making process. Your mentors and lending team members will help you determine what best fits you, as revealed in Step 5. That says it all. Every step in this process is invaluable in launching into real estate investing.

Now that you have mapped a source of financing, you need to raise cash for reserves and down payment. How exactly can you go about doing that? Step 7 helps realize that.

## 7. Raising Cash for Reserves and Down Payment

As a business, real estate provides the luxury of making use of others' money to drive you forward. Nevertheless, you should not bank on that, and must have some money down. You still need cash for reserves, even if you make use of any high leverage such as VA loans. How much is needed, and how can you raise it to get going?

First, the amount needed depends on your cash strategy and target market, as well as your property criteria. You can also inquire from any member of your lending team how much down payment is needed for certain loan programs. Here are a few ways to go about finding money:

- ➢ Save – As obvious as this is, it is worth mentioning. Cut down expenses, work to increase income, and hang in there until you have the money saved. It has no shortcuts but is highly effective.
- ➢ Borrow –You must take caution when borrowing. It is safer borrowing against rental properties and other long-term assets. Borrowing with personal loans, lines of credit and credit cards as down payments is often risky, especially when things turn out badly.
- ➢ Sell – Selling a personal item and purchasing a less expensive one is another way to raise the needed cash. Remember that you can always replace the item with something way better when you have the financial means to do so. You can use this same principle in terms of selling off an older home with lots of equity. By doing this you can also collect some additional funds selling off the junk collection in the garage, attic, or basement. You should not shy away from this option, as it remains one of the most logical and safest means to source for funds.
- ➢ Partner –Partnering has proven to be successful in delivering the goods, even when you cannot afford it in its entirety. All you need is to look for someone with money, who is interested in the collective cause, to put in a share and receive a part of the product. But you must be mindful of your level of communication. Every agreed term must be put down in writing and stated clearly. Work with people you trust and like to make the process much easier for you by reducing mental stress arising from distrust.

At this point, you have successfully lined up the cash and

financing needed to begin your real estate investing. It is time to find deals—I mean good deals!

## 8. Devise a Plan That Gets Deals

Think of this process as a treasure hunt, because good deals do not fall on your laps. Just as with a treasure hunt, where you have to scour an area and turn several stones over before you get the priceless gems you seek, you have to do some digging. But a plan—a great plan—will help you reach your target with ease. You must stick to your investment criteria to avoid being swayed by the market trends. Here are two steps to realize great deals in real estate:

> Marketing Budget

Your marketing budget can influence the deals you get in different ways. Although having a large budget lets you get much done with little effort, having nothing to start with still works. If your marketing budget is set at $0, creativity and plenty of personal time to do the footwork is required. As exhausting as that sounds, it can still fetch you results. If you have a few bucks in hand for marketing, you can tailor some marketing campaigns to suit your budget, as well. There is no doubt that having a decent marketing budget will set you apart from the competition.

One of your best ROI will often be your marketing investment. Still, you must critically examine what suits you most, even when you have the bucks needed to carry out campaigns.

➤ Marketing Campaign

There is no exact science to marketing as effective campaigns often change. As there are several marketing campaigns available to you, all you have to do is test them out and make a decision on the one that works for you. In an order of cost, here are some effective campaigns you can look to explore:

➤ Free to Low-Cost Marketing Campaigns

- Referral and Networking Campaign – Request prospective property leads from everyone you know. Discuss with family and friends, and expand your outreach to your professional contacts, including your attorney, CPA, real estate agents, financial advisers and property managers, etc. Network via meetings with landlords or other real estate or business meetings.
- Find Bird Dogs and Wholesalers – Some people in the industry are in business to help other investors find deals. Wholesalers and bird dogs are similar. Wholesalers control or buy deals and quickly resell for small markups, while bird dogs bring leads your way. It becomes your job to convert such leads to paying deals. To pay a bird dog a finder's fee often requires that they own a real estate license.
- MLS Campaign – Get a buyer's agent to send leads your way, depending on your criteria. The agents make use of a multiple listing service (MLS) to set up automatic emails delivered to your inbox when a reduced or new property reaches the market. Such deals often require

that you move fast on them, as virtually everyone else has this in motion.

- Classified Ads – Classified ads offer another free to low-cost platform to market your services. These can be found in local print or online publications.

- Cold Calling – This can be effective for people who can withstand a thousand rejections to make one successful call. To make this more effective, you need to get a listing of sales and rent owners from the local newspaper or online classifieds. Next, you have to start calling the numbers on the list and make inquiries. There is potential in this form of marketing, as many people pass up this option.

- Drive for Dollars – Driving through your neighborhood or doing a regular walk-through can fetch you deals. While on your drive, look out for vacant properties, "For Sale" or "For Rent" signs. Call the numbers on signs and speak to agents or owners when you can. When you see a vacant property, you can reach out to the neighbors to get information about the owner and when to reach them. You can also take the vacant house address down and search for the contact information of the owner, using a local tax accessor record or an online phone listing. You can choose to call or send a mail to inquire about purchasing their house.

➢ Intermediate and High-Cost Campaigns

- Direct Mail – Sending postcards or letters to several property owners is an alternative plan to get deals, but it comes at a cost. First, you must pay a local service or list company for a list to send direct mail. It can be a difficult route to secure deals, as a few investors follow through this channel. Still, you can secure deals here.

- Car Signs – A vinyl or magnetic lettering attached to your car can be a source to get deals. Write out a clear message and include your phone number. Although it breaks into your comfort zone, it is relatively cheap.

- Social Media and Website – A social media channel and website can perform wonders for you. They serve as business cards that can reach thousands of audiences and pull potential paying clients to you. Ensure that it conveys your message clearly—include who you are, your real estate investing business, what you are looking for, and what services you offer. As much as possible, create many contact lines to help people reach you.

- Advertising – This covers both traditional advertising forms and online advertising. Newspapers, community bulletins, talk radio, magazines, and Google AdWords are different means of advertising that can spread the word about your real estate investment business. Advertising costs can quickly spiral out of control, but with proper testing, it can provide a great ROI.

- Yard Signs – This is an effective means for lead generation, and it is not expensive. If allowed by the local municipal law, when renting or selling a house, put up a sign indicating that you rent or sell houses.

## Making a Decision

Deciding which marketing campaign to use is really up to you, as there are tons of marketing campaigns to explore and get results. It is also determined by your budget, but the methods mentioned above are some of the effective options available to you. Make a rough budget and decide on two campaigns to set out with.

## 9. Scheduling Time and Prioritizing Actions

Now is the time to take action. First, you must schedule your time, then prioritize. This will help your real estate investing get started as soon as possible.

➤ Scheduling Your Time

You know your time best, and how to schedule it to get the most of real estate investing. But you must pay attention to some things, as you likely will be busy. First, you must determine how much time you can set aside each week for this business. After allocating a set time for the business on a weekly basis, you must be realistic to sail through with ease. Ruthlessness with your priority list is required if you attach much value to your real· estate investing business. Remember that this business will not last until eternity; you have to make the most of what you have. More time is required from you at the initial stages, but it gets better as you build momentum. You can purchase properties and create systems when the momentum is right.

At the initial stages, you should be willing to invest about 10 hours of your time each week to grow your business and give yourself a chance to be successful in it. You also have to carve out time from your calendar to put some work into the business. Scheduling it makes it a priority.

> Prioritizing Your Next Steps

There is a difference between time management and action management. Getting your projects done is not about time management, but rather action management. This simply means that you must spend time doing things that drive you towards your goals.

One big way to realize this has been hinted earlier in Chapter 3. You have to break large tasks in bits, keeping them in a checklist. Do this for now:

> Identify Your Next Projects: Put down in writing some projects that must be finalized for your real estate investment to commence. Projects contain steps, and this chapter is a project on its own. If you do not know where to start, reviewing this chapter from the beginning will put you on track.

> Know Your Next Line of Action: Put in writing the next few actions needed to move the above-mentioned project forward. You can use your next scheduled time for real estate investing to do this.

> Act! Act! Act!: Do what you have written as your next line of action. Either act within the allocated time, or right now.

> Repeat the Process: Repeat until you complete the entire goal of beginning real estate investing. Actions will keep coming up until you can complete a project. On completing that task, get into the next thing on the list.

These nine steps will save you the time and frustration of not getting in touch with your goal of investing in the real estate business. Now that you have made strides toward progress, you need to continue the process. It is one thing to start and a different thing to continue the process. The next chapter will help you keep up with the process and actualize your real estate investing goal.

**Notes**

_____

_____

_____

_____

**Daily wins or accomplishments**

_____

_____

_____

_____

_____

_____

_____

CHAPTER 6

# ACCOUNTABILITY

ACCOUNTABILITY IS ONE OF the most important parts of this diet. This is why people have a mentor, personal trainer, or a coach. Many people fail because they don't have someone in their ear, or to check in with when times get tough. Early on in real estate investing, a lot of people seek mentors or gurus to learn from, but after they have learned, there is usually a drop-off in the commitment to what they have learned. This is because people don't know where to start, or lose motivation if they aren't seeing results quick enough. It then becomes a waste of time and money. These patterns turn cyclical for people that attend multiple seminars that provide the same content on the same subject. The hardest part about going through these programs is that you leave with a ton of knowledge and don't know where to start, so you give up. They give you the knowledge, but not a roadmap or a plan on how to execute what you learned. They also don't check in to see what you need help with, or if you are applying what you have learned.

Now that you've set a goal, what else is there for you to do? What is expected of you, and what should be done differently to accomplish your target? Has the lack of achievement resulted in disappointment and are you weary of moving your goals into another year, in spite of being hopeful that something might change sooner? Taking the time to consider how to realize your goals is something everyone who aspires to be successful would do. Just as starting out with passion is important in achieving your goal to supplement your income, so is the implementation of your action plan. Whether you are a self-starter or have a team to work with, the initial belief that you can see the goal through often fades out when your plan of action is yet to be implemented. The huge task of enforcing the entire plan from start to completion seems way beyond your scope.

There are several factors that may be responsible for this, yet accountability—that is, a lack of it—is a major factor preventing you from reaching your goal. Research has revealed that a goal shared with others is easier to be achieved than a goal kept to yourself.

Accountability in this scenario refers to being held responsible for your goals. In terms of tracking the rate of success, accountability has no negative connotation. It creates a sense of pride and ownership, which often leads to greater achievement. Accountability separates the mediocre from the extremely successful. Trying to reach a certain goal all by yourself with no assistance whatsoever might end up with no actual result.

Let's take a cue from a health situation. Studies reveal that people who transition into healthier lifestyles are people who join some form of accountability program. This includes hiring a nutritionist or trainer, or joining a fitness club. The idea is simply answering to someone else for actions that keep you in line with the progress of your goal.

Just as accountability is needed to achieve health, it also applies to business activities. The level of success you achieve heavily depends on the accountability system you have set in place. Someone is needed to take up your dream, scale it up into goals, strategize, and execute the plan. Otherwise, you stand the risk of getting no result in the foreseeable future. You must have someone in your influence circle that is trustworthy, whom you can fill in about your goals. Enlist help from someone who has achieved something similar to what you're setting out to do. Signing up for a personal coaching program, joining a group session, or enlisting the services of a coach to gain accountability is common practice among successful people.

Here are five reasons why you should avail yourself of this vital component of success.

## 1. Performance Acceleration

One advantage of accountability is that it accelerates your performance. If you are in search of tangible progress in your endeavors, you must not neglect this. Connecting with a coach, on a personal level or in a group, can finesse your plans, help adjust and improve your strategy, and eventually lead to a winning execution pathway. Speaking of execution, there is added confidence when you are mentored through a process, compared to doing it all by yourself. So, you can rest assured that having this component of success in place will ensure the execution of your plan with confidence.

## 2. A Great Measure of Progress and Success

What is success like, and how can it be measured? A great coach will define this. You will also learn how to track your progress. Knowing what metrics are involved in measuring your success will give you a fair idea of where you stand in realizing your goals and what is needed to get to that point. It is key to seeing the overall picture going on around you.

## 3. Breeding Engagement

Life is filled with distractions. To succeed, you must learn to shut out the noise and focus on where you are headed. As there are lots of things to pull you off course, accountability drives engagement. Fatigue, boredom, or any form of distraction may tend to set you off the pace, but remembering that you are accountable to someone ensures you stay on track and complete the course.

## 4. Keeping Yourself Responsible

Working with a coach who drives you through tremendous change in a short time with efficient results will lead to the realization that the bulk of the load lies at your feet. When you are to deliver tangible results on a weekly basis, and the efforts put into realizing your goals are commensurate with the result, you will know that it is up to you to drive progress. Such realization is the effect of accountability. Accounting to others for every step taken will help you foster a serious mindset, approach, and work ethic aimed at reaching your objective. You will take a proper look at yourself and your actions, rid yourself of every excuse that hampers your progress, and take deliberate steps to attain success.

## 5. Validation of Your Ideas and Thoughts

Self-criticism can be a hindrance to success, especially when it is unbalanced. Accounting to someone else can reduce the volume of your inner critic. Moreover, using someone as a screen who is apt at making sound decisions will go a long way in helping you build confidence in your own thoughts and ideas, apart from the validation of your thinking process. Therefore, choosing the right coach or partner is integral in driving accountability. How you go about that will be discussed subsequently.

Now that we have seen some major reasons why you must hold yourself accountable to the goals you set, it is vital that you know the types of accountability. This will help you decide what you must do to make the most of your goals.

## Ways to Stay Accountable

Being accountable to your goals is a broad subject. Depending on your personality and what you set out to do, some types of accountability will work better than others. You can try them all out and combine a few that suit you. Below are a few that I found to be most beneficial for keeping me accountable.

> ➤ Inform a friend
> ➤ Join a support group
> ➤ Write down
> ➤ Hire a coach
> ➤ Make use of technology.

## Inform a Friend in Real Estate

Telling someone who cares can really help you attain what you aspire to. This individual will be ready to speak with you about your goals, help you achieve them, and celebrate your wins when you reach a milestone. Picking the right accountable partner is also important. Not just anyone will do. Someone who gets overcompetitive or would water down your efforts is capable of sabotaging your success. The ideal partner is someone who is fully on board with you, someone who is your fan through and through.

## Join a Mastermind Group

Mastermind groups are great centers to keep yourself account-able to your goals. Since accountability is a two-way street, you can create a group or join one that you can relate with. You will be helped to achieve feats that you cannot reach on your own when you associate with a support group. Seeing others achieve a feat of interest inspires you to do the same. This is why joining a book club or writing group is so effective. Man is a social being; we help others and can be helped to reach our goals. When we avail ourselves of such relationships, we achieve our goals faster than we do going solo.

## Write It Down

Traits differ from person to person. For some, writing down their aspirations is enough to bring it to life. Others need to do something extra to get things going. Writing your goal down can strengthen your resolve in completing a difficult task. Posting a checklist at a visible site, where it is obvious to you, is one way to go about the process effectively. But it all depends on you to figure out what works best for you. Regardless of your decision, the fact remains that writing your goals down is one of the easiest ways to realize your dreams. All you have to do is post reminders and use checklists such as daily planners, notes on your computer's desktop, or wall calendar.

## Hire a Coach

Coaching is on the rise as never before, and this is all for its perks. With the help of a coach, your goals become clear to you, and you are held accountable to a specified timeline to achieve your objectives. There are even more benefits to hiring a coach. This individual is experienced in whatever particular area of interest that you would like coached and will help you circumvent a challenge that poses a threat to reaching the desired objective. Coaching is a means of self-reporting and a tool to measure your actions. Great coaches never blame, scold, or judge; they are there to help you realize what will help you meet your personal commitments and what will not. That point should linger in your mind when choosing a coach.

## Make Use of Technology

Technology can be handy in keeping you accountable to your goals. Many websites and apps are specifically designed to help track your progress or offer reminders of the goals you set for yourself. Some apps or websites can even connect you with like-minded individuals who are passionate about a similar cause. It is really up to you to decide what tech platform you prefer to use and how well you can utilize it. The ultimate goal is to get productive and reach your goals and if an app or website will help you remain accountable, then it is a good choice.

## How to Determine If You're Better Off Without an Accountability Partner

There is little argument that you sometimes need external help in your journey to supplement your income. More is often achieved with an accountability setup in place, and most times, the different types of accountability do overlap. Nevertheless, each accountability type is designed to fulfill a need at a certain point. Understanding what each brings to the table will shape your decision at any given point.

The major point here is deciding which type of accountability to use. A coach might be the best option if you aim at accelerating your learning curve, since he has gone through the exact path you intend to, and has honed the skills needed to navigate it.

A mastermind group gives you something different. If you are up for the challenge and would like to roll with others, build connections that you lack at present, and observe people's struggles from another perspective, then this might suit you more.

Having an accountability partner helps when you know what to do, but discover that you are not meeting your own expectations. It might be your best bet for disciplining yourself.

However, you may be a very private person and would like to go solo in reaching your goals. You might not be comfortable expressing your worries, pains, achievement and struggles with others. Using an app or website to track your development may be all you need to account for the goals set by you.

Whatever type of accountability you choose, the underlying principle is to set yourself up in a situation that ensures that you keep working toward your goals. When you have that in place, things will begin to flow for you.

## What You Must Know About Having a Partner

There is no doubting that getting a partner will help you get stuff done. But you must know that simply having a partner will not automatically translate into success, it's not that straightforward. Just as you can accomplish great feats with your partner, you can also find yourself on the opposite end of the curve. Experience has shown me that it is common practice to pick a friend when selecting an accountability partner. However, sometimes that can be dangerous. There are several situations where an individual has to look elsewhere for another partner because the relationship does not drive the required discipline to get stuff done. Not only is this a waste of precious time, but that setback can affect your career path and eventually lead to a loss of focus. No one would ever want that. So here are seven points to note about having an accountability partner. Trust me! You will come out all the better because of it.

## 1. Having Multiple Accountability Partners Is a Great Idea

Do you have several tasks you want to accomplish? If so, a single accountability partner may not be right for you. Sticking to one person to help you navigate terrain they are unfamiliar with is likely to have a disastrous end. There is no rule forbidding having multiple partners. You just have to make sure that all your accountability partners are accomplished in the areas you need them for. Do not select an individual for just any reason; you should be picking them for the value they present to you, which is to grow.

## 2. Your Partner Can Be Miles Away From You

You do not have to be in the same city as your accountability partner. There are different means to track your goals, even from a distance. You can choose to connect via Skype, Zoom, or any other technological route. The exciting thing is that your accountability partner can reside anywhere on the planet, and you can do just fine.

## 3. Identify Your Preferred Channel of Communication

Regardless of how near or far your accountability partner is to you, you must identify the communication channel that suits both parties best. Would you or your partner prefer a face-to-face meeting, text, email, Skype meeting, or a blend of all? There must be a mutual understanding of what suits you both. This will limit the feeling of inconvenience from any side. Only after ensuring that everyone is comfortable with the platform for sharing and receiving ideas can you progress to your goals.

## 4. Timing

Just as you both must agree on the communication channel that works best, you must also decide on the timing of your meetings. Both parties must agree upon a day and time that is convenient to get the best results. When there is a need to switch things up, it must be agreed upon by everyone involved. The communication line must always be open.

## 5. Advance Preparation

Time is of the essence, and the manner in which you present yourself leaves a lasting impression on your partners. Partners don't want to collaborate if they know their assistance is going to be needed all the time, if that is the case an individual wouldn't want a partner up as the advantage or benefit they are desiring is lost. It's not saving them time and it's more work on their part. One way to show your desire is to prepare in advance. Sending your partner a list of your goals will help you jump right in when you meet. It eliminates time loss, and gives the impression of how serious you are about reaching your goals.

## 6. Express Yourself

Sometimes you might observe that you and your partner(s) are not moving at the same pace. You may also be the silent or the shy type who does not want to speak up. At such times, you just have to push yourself and let your partner know that you are not in sync. If there is a need for adjustment, you must air your views. After trying all you can, if you still observe there is not much improvement in the communication line or other areas of the relationship, do not hesitate to look elsewhere for an accountability partner who can facilitate the realization of your goals.

## 7. Honesty

Working with an accountability partner is not the time to hide your weaknesses and promote your strengths. You must be honest with them about your abilities, weaknesses, or challenges. Only then can you receive the help and guidance that you need.

## What to Do With Your Accountability Partner

Most people endlessly talk about their dreams, hopes, and desires. But days turn into months, and years go by without making any actionable progress, putting the ambition to a halt. We often procrastinate and fail to act towards our goals.

Even though you possess a great idea and brim with ambition

and talent, without putting these qualities to the test, no one will ever find out if you can succeed. Therein lies the major reason why you need to seek ways to be accountable. Accountability directs you towards your goals; it pushes you until you reach your dream. Your performance is accelerated through consistent, steady progress. To be accountable to the goals you set, here is what you need to do.

## 1. Stick to a Schedule

A common error is to set a deadline for ourselves to achieve a goal. We set these deadlines without paving a way to realize our goals by the set date. We are so engrossed with the desired outcome that we forget that a goal is achieved through a series of related processes. Whatever it is that we wish, dream of, or think about has no influence if there is no commitment to achieving steady progress. Things do not just happen magically; you must realize that it all starts with you.

Sticking to a schedule is essential; you cannot avoid it. A schedule forms the basis of your game plan and helps you evaluate how consistent you are toward your goal. A great schedule should be clearly designed and time-focused within reasonable and attainable limits. It will help you scale up smaller goals and translate bigger ones into actionable steps.

For instance, maybe you aim to increase your following and grow your client base. This goal requires that you create a schedule to connect with your audience on a consistent basis, let's say weekly. Whatever happens during your week, make sure it does not pass by without you reaching out to your clients. Follow through with the process, and once there is consistency, you will draw ever closer to your goal.

## 2. Be Honest with Yourself

Everyone has something to offer. Still, we cannot be experts in every field. For instance, some people are more comfortable channeling their thoughts via writing, and struggle with in-person conversation, while for others it is the other way around. Setting goals in areas of weakness will be counterproductive. Ensure that you set goals that develop and emphasize your strengths, as well as relegate your weaknesses.

Making an honest appraisal of yourself involves identifying your talents and shortcomings, and accepting what works best for you under certain conditions. Knowing your limits will set you up for success in realizing your goals.

There is more. You must identify the environment that suits you best, as well as the conditions that limit your abilities. Look for how to increase efficiency and focus in your weak areas, and isolate the factors that keep you on track with your goals.

## 3. Break Down Your Goals

When I speak of breaking down your goals, I do not refer to tossing your dreams aside or dreaming less. After all, we are all encouraged to dream big and you really should. You are the only one who knows the exact extent of your dream, and you have set out to see it through. But even when you have a schedule in place to actualize the process, you may still feel overwhelmed by the huge size of the task. Don't worry; this is a phase we all go through. Picture your dream as a high mountain that you want to climb. Often, when people look at the mountain they have to climb, they plunge into deep procrastination as a result of the overwhelming outlook of what they have to do. Resist such an urge, and make yourself accountable by easing the workload. This is possible by taking baby steps in the direction of your goal.

This can be done by splitting each segment into "micro-goals." Each large task taking you in the direction of the goal can be broken down into small, progressive units in your schedule. You must keep slicing your goals into small chunks until they are easy to carry out. And as you carry out each step, do not forget to celebrate how far you have come. Celebrating your success will spur you on.

Much has been said about accountability, and by now it is glaringly obvious that it shares a relationship with progress. If you take each step of your goals with ease, as you aim to do, by splitting each large task, you are reducing your chance of getting overwhelmed by the enormous task. You also become more clinical in carrying out each smaller task ahead. While the feeling of achieving a long-term goal is often our sole focus, it is the little steps we take that really increase engagement and drive productivity and creativity.

## 4. Overcome Self-Sabotage

Our mind is a great tool that affects the outcome of our goals. Just as the subconscious layer of the mind can map things out for us, it can also limit our success. The fear of leaving our comfort zone is self-destructive and a dream killer. It is something you must be wary of. If you have fallen victim to a failed dream or ambition in the past by not following through on your goals, you might have a feeling of self-sabotage. But this feeling does not have to be repetitive. Being accountable will help you understand the actions that impede your progress. By identifying negative patterns, you will effectively overcome self-sabotage.

## 5. Have a Partner

This idea has been floated throughout this chapter, but what hasn't been mentioned is the dynamics involved in the partner role. You may easily conclude from what has been said that the accountability partner is a one-way street. That is not true—an accountability partner will drive you toward your goals, and you will do so for them in return. Instead of letting commitment slide by going solo in pursuing your goals, an accountability partner will help infuse consistency into your execution. A good partner brings commitment to the table. If the person you've partnered with is not reliable, then you should look elsewhere.

## 6. Identify Your "Why"

To hold yourself accountable to your goals, you must have a clear reason why the goal matters to you. How will reaching the goal add value to your existence, or to those around you? What is its purpose? Understanding the motivations behind each goal you set will improve your accountability to it.

Keep your reason at the top of your mind when embarking on the micro-steps leading to your goal. Continue educating yourself on the objectives of the goal and avoid acting contrary to it. Fill your mind with positivity by acquiring information and knowledge that will build your reasons for having the goal in the first place. This is how you build your focus.

Whenever an objective is set, you must consciously take the necessary steps to realize the goal in place. In all, to hold yourself accountable, you must deeply embrace every reason there is to achieve the goal. But remember, you cannot embrace what you do not know. Hence, it all starts with knowledge. Keep feeding the dream.

## 7. Celebrate Little Wins

You might wonder what celebration has to do with holding yourself accountable to your goals. The answer is that it reinforces your sense of accomplishment. Whether little or huge, you must not disregard each step taken to reach your goals. Celebrating little wins builds confidence and momentum, and enables you to maintain focus on the larger picture.

When talking about celebrating, I'm not speaking of a grand gesture, such as throwing a party. Instead, celebrate your little wins in small and relevant ways that imprint the moment in your memory. Write down your daily successes, or even the little steps you have taken to accomplish your goals on a weekly basis. This largely depends on you and your schedule. Regardless of which time frame you use to accomplish your little goals and paste the success list where it is visible to you every day. Ensure you keep piling up the list, so you can have a preview of how far you have come in reaching your goal.

Note that your dreams are just dreams until you write them down—only then do they become goals! Having a master list where all your macro- and micro-goals are penned down is a must. It helps you account for your goals. Once you accomplish each task, cross it off your list. If it is something you would want others to know about, you can opt to share it on your social media channels. Sharing your achievements with friends and family opens the opportunity to be cheered on by onlookers. Just take a look at how athletes value the input of spectators to boost their morale. That is exactly what you get when you let others be part of your journey.

## 8. Take Stock

Without reviewing your goals, you might just be traveling a directionless journey. Reviewing how well you are doing at each stage gives you a picture of your overall progress. The interesting part of this phase of being accountable is that it can help you find your feet when you backslide, help maintain consistency, and spur you to move into top gear.

Looking at how you are performing with your schedule and how you are completing your micro- and macro-goals is a good point to start from. Next, you should ensure your accountability partner is performing well in keeping you on track. Is your work of good quality, and are you pleased with what you are currently doing to realize your goals? If not, you must seek areas to improve. If your motivation is slipping, you also have to work on that. But you must maintain the air of positivity, as this makes it easier to account for the goals you've set out to reach.

## Why Accountability Works

Holding yourself accountable for every goal you've set is a means of telling the universe that the goal is important to you. It is not something you are undecided about, but something you really want. Not making provisions to hold yourself accountable shows you are not serious. It is often very easy to let your dreams go as a result of being overwhelmed, but an accountability system ensures you stay on track and get the desired result.

One other reason why this system works so well is that it helps you save face. Reputation matters, and it is something we all care to protect. When reputation is on the line, it is human nature to do everything possible to make sure that we meet the expectations placed on us. That is exactly what an accountable partner brings to the table. Will you be seen as an indecisive individual with no follow through or someone who lacks integrity to get things accomplished? That is one question that comes to mind when you hold yourself accountable to your goals. And you can imagine what the outcome of your experience will be with such a mindset. Also, remember that when the heat is turned up, having the right kind of support will see you through any sort of hurdle. That suggests once again the importance of having the right type of accountability partner. With the right partner, you always have a cheerleader around to remind you of your potential, as well as how far you have come.

No matter our personality, past achievements or status, we all need a system to help us account for our pursuits. Procrastination is a goal-killer that is always ready to pounce on productivity. But it will be put in the right position in our orbit with an accountability partner. If you are intent on getting things done, you must not overlook the need to hold yourself accountable to your goals.

**Notes**

_____

_____

_____

_____

**Daily wins or accomplishments**

_____

_____

_____

_____

_____

_____

_____

CHAPTER 7

# REAL ESTATE MILLIONAIRE SECRETS

IN JUST 90 DAYS from now, your bank account can go from having monthly overdraft fees to monthly deposits ranging from $4,500 to $30,000 or more, with just the purchase of a $100 booklet of stamps. If you can't afford stamps, ask someone to buy you some. It's a tasteful way of asking for cash so you don't come off like you need a handout. Also, you won't feel like you owe anyone money and will have good energy behind what you're doing with the stamps. Yes, all you need is stamps—no money! This is the genesis of making money in real estate for free. There is no ceiling on the amount of income you can generate, once you learn and apply what I've showed you throughout this book. Knowledge is power, but only when it is used!

In writing this book, I wanted to do everything I could to make sure you're ready to be wealthy from real estate. But it's up to you to take action and apply the principles I shared with you. I understand how mentally tough it can be to break away from the monotony of life, but if you've picked up this book, you've already taken the first step in changing your life. That was an obstacle I faced, so I dedicated a chapter to mental preparation, the most important part of becoming wealthy. I also wanted to mix in a little inspiration to keep you motivated on your path to make real estate investing your day job in less than 90 days.

Ask yourself, "WHY real estate?" Is it for the dream, the money, to be financially independent, to not have to work for someone else the rest of your life? Most millionaires have their "whys" with real estate, but I'm going to give you the main components as to why people become wealth investing in real estate.

These are the five key factors in why wealthy people choose real estate as their main vehicle of choice in terms of investing to build long term wealth:

1. Appreciation
2. Cash flow
3. Loan debt paid down by a tenant
4. Amazing tax benefits
5. Inflation hedge if you tie up fixed long-term interest rate debt

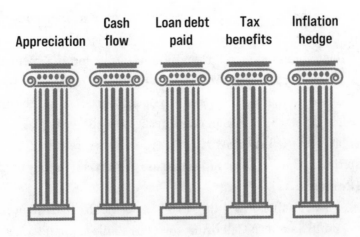

Appreciation | Cash flow | Loan debt paid | Tax benefits | Inflation hedge

These are the fundamental advantages of investing in real estate and should provide more clarity as to why and how so many people became millionaires investing in real estate and the method to possibly amassing large sums of income passively. It's not a secret, but it is the pillar of why this is the investment vehicle of choice for the wealthy. Based on these five fundamentals, it's clear that real estate is not a way to get rich overnight. You must have a vision in order to reap the long-term benefits of real estate investing.

## The Importance of Vision

Life is all about vision. Think of driving a car at night without headlights illuminating the road. Without vision, you can't see what's in front of you and don't know where you're going. What tends to happen if you don't know where you're going?

The only way you got to where you are today is by envisioning yourself being there. Good or bad, your thoughts led you there.

because that is the only possible way you could get there, unless you were physically forced.

The millionaire secret is envisioning. **"A vision is a picture of a preferred future."** You have to practice visualization and master it so that when it's time to open your eyes, your brain will bring you back to your actual reality. Use the principles that apply with the Law of Attraction, or for anyone reading that is spiritual, **"Speak those things that are not as though they are." (Romans 4.17).**

As I write this, I'm sitting in a $3,000/month apartment in beautiful Southern California, not even a mile from the beach. I'm not saying this to brag, but only to say I envisioned myself living in this exact complex when I first moved to California. I couldn't afford to live here at that time, and I actually just stumbled upon the area when I was searching Craigslist to find a room to rent. As I passed the location I'm in now, I said, "I'm going to live there one day," because it was right by the beach and had a really nice sportsplex across the street. Three and a half years later, I was living in that exact building. Months before that, I printed out a photo of a car that I wanted and put it on my vision board. Four months later, I went to a dealership and test-drove a car that I liked. They didn't have any models available that I wanted, but more were being delivered in a few weeks. I told the salesman, "As long as it's white, I'm fine." They delivered the car to my home, and as I went to put the date I acquired the car on the image on my vision board, I read the specs of my "dream car" and it was the exact car—same color, same features, same interior—that I put on my board four months prior.

I share these stories to let you know that nothing is impossible. I spent a huge portion of my childhood growing up with six people in two-bedroom house with a tin roof, built by my grand-father and cousin. (To put into perspective how big the house is, when I go into that house now, I hit my head on the ceiling.) We grew up on food stamps and whatever my grandmother could grow in her small garden. Everyone in my neighborhood and school lived just like us, and as a kid, I thought this was how life is everywhere, until one day I had a chance to see something different. I was never the same again. I could only dream of the life I have now, but I envisioned myself living that way. real estate made it possible for me, and I want to make it possible for you.

If you're serious about doing something that could help you live the life you desire, please refocus your attention and apply what was given to you in this book.

## Four Key Components to Success

Over the course of generations, real estate has generated more millionaires than any other investment vehicle. Unless you capitalized on the tech boom or are great at day-trading or doing options, real estate is the only investment vehicle that can yield 1000 percent return in 45 days or less. Real estate statistically has created more wealth for most multi-millionaires, aside from those who capitalized on the tech boom and those who are currently active in the tech space i.e. Google, Facebook, Snapchat, and Airbnb, to name a few.

Remember, there are four key components for any business to be successful:

1. Need
2. Cost
3. Profitability
4. Sustainability

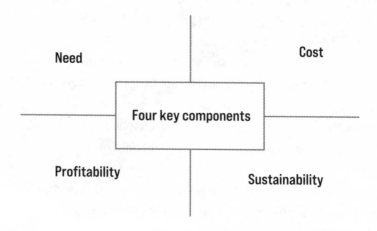

Need

Cost

Four key components

Profitability

Sustainability

Would you agree that everyone will always need a place to live? Whether it's an apartment or a house, one thing is constant: we all need a place to call home. Owning real estate, be it commercial or residential, meets the four key components you need to be successful in business.

I bet you're thinking, "But what if the economy is bad? Then you can't sell or buy houses." You are wrong! But if you are thinking that, then those are the results you're going to get. I'm sure you've heard the saying *You are what you eat*; well, you are what you think. So how about we just dispel that belief right now.

In any economic climate, has the entire country ever stopped living in homes or apartments? Will there or has there ever been 100 percent employment? Will people stop getting fired? Are people going to start living forever? Do real estate investors stop looking for properties to buy?

If you answered "yes" to any of those questions, don't start this diet, because real estate is not for you. In any economic climate, real estate will be bought and sold at a discount, and people who have the knowledge from this book will be the ones buying it and making enormous amounts of money, because they know how to find deals. Out of those five questions how many do you think could potentially be motivated sellers? In any economic situation!

Did we just dispel the thought that you can't sell or buy houses in any economic situation?

People think millionaires are the only ones who can make money in a down economy, so they make no attempt to look for properties, thinking they are all gone. Take for instance Augusta, Georgia, where I and one of my business partners buy a lot of properties. Every Thursday morning, the local newspaper publishes a foreclosure list with names and addresses included. These properties are scheduled to be sold at auction on the courthouse steps on the first Tuesday of the following month. This list can have anywhere between 30 and 70 names of people who are about to lose their home in 30 days.

Our first few deals came from this list, and many of our deals to this day still come from the same newspaper. The first deal from the list yielded us $3,000, which we just put back into marketing. I know you're thinking, "Oh, that's not a lot of money," but you have to get a few wins under your belt to get the confidence for tackling bigger deals when they come. Remember, something is better than nothing, and you need to practice your craft. Michael Jordan didn't hit a game winner his first time in a game. Most people would have moved on to something that may yield a better payout and miss out on a great opportunity because they only made $3,000, but guess what? Our next deal from that same newspaper list yielded us $35,000. It gets even better: we didn't use any of our own money at all. We didn't even spend money on stamps. The power of door knocking is pretty amazing. Are you starting to see how you make millions in real estate? In what other business can you make millions of dollars without spending any money?

In any economic climate, in any state, the components of a successful real estate business do not change what you've been taught on how to find the right properties with no money!

I know it's hard to grasp, but I've given you the courage to step outside of your comfort zone and take action. Confidence comes from being fully equipped with the wealth of real estate investing knowledge you've learned from reading this book. Follow the diet like your life depends on it, because it does.

**Notes**

_____

_____

_____

_____

**Daily wins or accomplishments**

_____

_____

_____

_____

_____

_____

_____

# CONCLUSION

MY PERSONAL EXPERIENCE SHOWS how possible it is to invest in real estate. You can do this, as well. Supplementing your income in the next 90 days is realistic—in fact, you can be kicking your boss out. This real estate investing diet simplifies how building a net worth of over a million dollars is attainable.

Whatever you do, getting results makes the difference, and the type of diet you use matters. The result often varies from person to person, but following this diet step by step gives the desired result. As I mentioned earlier, I have been able to increase my net worth solely in real estate to over $1.2 million, and did so without using my own money. I am 100 percent positive that it will work that way for you. Remember how my story started. Life was a rollercoaster, yet I worked through it. My past did not dictate my future success, and you should not let it dictate yours.

Being rich and successful is not luck. You must follow the lead of other successful people. I hope that you followed the suggestions mentioned in the introductory words of this book, to take your first steps into real estate only when you have completed the steps in the first two chapters.

Along with productive habits, being coachable and disciplined set me up for success. Total commitment is expected from you to realize the intent of this book, as it outlines something different from other diets you might have come across.

The first strides to follow this diet, especially in the next 90 days, are to embark on marketing, get homes under contract, and assign homes to a buyer for a fee. Wholesaling is the only exit strategy you should be using for the next 60 to 120 days. This will drive you closer to your real estate investing goals in the shortest time possible.

My hope is that you apply this diet starting today and avoid any form of procrastination. Most people will move when they will begin these steps; others will use the never-ending tomorrow, and eventually, they will toss the knowledge away. So you must start now. If you are not totally on board with this diet, do not expect to be fully nourished. For those who will take this half-heartedly and still complain it does not work for them, it is best you correct that from the onset and adopt every bit of it.

Any diet gives temporary results until it is made a way of life. Remember that, as it is your best chance of transforming your life. Stick with the process and be consistent. There is an expiration date for every diet, but with the right mindset, you can transform this into a lifestyle and keep getting results.

You will discover that real estate is a great investment if you invest much time in educating yourself on how it works and the best methods of increasing returns. However, a lot of people with an interest in making an investment in real estate or purchasing a rental property do not often do so. People who do not avail themselves of learning about real estate investment miss out on different levels. Apart from making real wealth, the satisfaction of growing a business is missing. In fact, real estate investing actualizes the goal of being financially independent. Just take a look at the stock market. This investment vehicle, which we were taught to see as the best mode of investment, demands we invest money and watch as stocks rise. And therein lies the problem—all we usually do is depend solely on our stocks' value to rise. The stock market determines retirement calculators, which help us guess how much to save, based on when we will die. We are either saving too little or saving too much on such calculations. With real estate investing, it is not the same. Real estate investing is all about the cash flow. Cash flow increases with time, while your investment principal remains intact. Real estate investing can be compared to that stock with high dividends, one where you have no worries about the value of the stock rising for a great return on investment.

The one thing all successful people share is mental conditioning. This is the most important part of making it big in your real estate investing. Successful people are committed to excellence and avoid doing things on autopilot. They put in concrete efforts to avoid lackluster results. They understand that life really starts where our comfort zone ends. Thriving in an uncomfortable zone makes life outside that zone easier. Always remember that you cannot improve and not change at the same time.

Most people are mentally conditioned by their circumstances. Their background and neighborhood can shape the strength of their mental conditioning, whether weak or strong. This is an important aspect you must consider in staying on track with your goal of success in real estate investing. You need to have a measure of relentlessness, which strong mental conditioning promotes. Such relentlessness will not only block the external noise, but will also keep you calm through the process. Your first deal may not come at once, as I mentioned in Chapter 1; it may take up to two years of consistent effort. Many people have attested to this experience. Without the right mental conditioning to withstand this, they likely would have given up. Missed opportunity, lack of funding, and seeing sellers back out of deals can be discouraging and put you off the path. But with the right mindset, you can see the process through and come out on top.

Naysayers also make it difficult to achieve success in real estate investing. You must look out and avoid such people. Successful people have mentally conditioned themselves to know that failure is necessary, because if you are not failing, then you are not trying.

Planted seeds require time to sprout. To achieve real estate investing success, you must believe you can. You just have to set standards. Feeding on the wrong diet is killing millions around the world. But what kills more is what is eating them. Many people do not believe that they can actually pull this off even if they subscribe to tons of programs and seminars on how they can take charge of their lives. This diet helps you adopt the proper mindset, become an entrepreneur in the most real sense, and make money out of it.

Stretch yourself to grow, put in the work, and be accountable. If you cannot discipline yourself, it is best to seek the assistance of others. Your accountability partner will help you navigate hurdles and ensure your goals become a reality. Continual evaluation is needed as well, to check and monitor your progress. Be quick to take reactionary measures when you spot that you are falling out of line. People who wait do not get what they dream of. It is up to you to break through barriers in the right direction. And that is what this diet describes in its entirety.

Having the right mindset drives you toward success. People who have made a success from real estate investing view money differently than most. Most people are quick to spend money immediately when they receive a tax return or get a raise. Whereas, the really rich ones invest and cut costs. Many people today find themselves in more debt than ever, and believe that a better job with improved pay is the only way to get rich. In reality, investing is what really brings wealth, and wealthy people know that for a fact. They not only *know*; they *do*. Action is what separates them from the people who only develop an interest but take no measurable step toward it. After setting out toward their goals, the wealthy maintain consistency through the odds, giving total commitment. You must ask yourself which group you belong to, and identify what group you would want to move into. Your current state does not reflect where you will end up. It all depends on what you do now! Remember, 80 percent of success is psychological and 20 percent is mechanics. Embrace the concept of achieving success in your mind, and work toward it. A stable flow of cash, diversification, leverage, and to top it all off, a source of passive income are the ultimate benefits you stand to gain when all your effort pays off. What better way could there by to realize your dreams than by doing something delightful? Only you can define your story.

# ACKNOWLEDGMENTS

FIRST, I'D LIKE TO thank my parents, Johnnie and Ella, for supporting me on my entrepreneurial path and encouraging me to write this book to share my expertise. They felt it could be a great guide and resource for people with a similar path to my own.

I also want to thank my friends and family for giving me purpose and motivation to complete this book and get it published. Thank you for sticking around when I disappeared for days at a time.

But I cannot express how grateful I am for those men and women who came into my life right when I needed them most over the years who saw something in me that I didn't see in myself. They shared their wisdom through talks, books, and by example for me and others trying to find their way.

To my son, Mason A. Stewart, you inspire me and make me want to be a better man—which in turn makes me a better leader. Thank you for being my ultimate inspiration for writing this book.

# ABOUT THE AUTHOR

Have you ever felt overwhelmed or depressed? Been homeless, unemployed, or on government assistance? That was André's life path before entering the world of finance. But everything changed when at the age of thirty-three, his doctor ordered him to quit working at his high-level bank position, where he was an advisor to CEOs of startups, major tech companies, and high net worth individuals. The stress was literally killing him, leaving André on the brink of cardiac arrest.

André then discovered the knowledge of real estate investing, and was able to achieve financial independence in less than seven months in that industry. Today, André is the founder and CEO of Residual Roads Business Institute and InvestFar, the latter being the first mobile app that lets you purchase, renovate, sell, or mange an investment property remotely.

Residing in Los Angeles, California, he enjoys traveling, playing basketball, and spending time with family and friends. His mission now is to help others from all walks of life discover mental awareness and financial independence.

# WHAT NOW?

Thank you for reading and starting this diet. To jump start the integration of what you have read and learned to reach your ninety-day goal, here are a list of things to do, preferably in this order:

1. **Download the Real Estate Investing app, InvestFar.**

By scanning the barcode on the back of this book, you will be led to the app store immediately so that you don't have to go searching for it. Please scan both codes to see which one applies to your device. This will give you instant access to all the tools and resources you need to Find & Evaluate, Acquire, Renovate, or Rent & Manage investment properties without some of the heavy lifting outlined in Chapter 4.

2. **Create a vision board.**

Vision boards will allow you to manifest the major wins and accomplishments as it activates your reticular activator on a daily basis, which trains your brain to consistently perform habits that bring to fruition the goals or things you have placed on the board. Focus all of your attention and energy toward this board for twenty minutes a day, or at minimum, once a week.

### 3. Download your daily planner.

Go to www.andrestewartauthor.com and input the requested information for you to receive your daily planner via email. Once you receive the planner, download and print it so you can put pen or paper on something tangible. This will help make you feel more accountable, as it requires you to complete a task or make notes every day.

### 4. Stick to your diet plan.

If you're reading this, it means you've followed step number 3 above and have a very detailed plan that will aid you in reaching all of your goals. Staying consistent and aggressive in your plan will allow your mind to be reconditioned and carry over into other aspects of your life. Prep for the next day in advance as the key is time management. If you plan ahead for the next day, your mind will expend less effort if you fall behind on time or something unexpected pops up. Always remember you are not alone and anyone can do this.

Support is always needed, no matter what level of success you reach. Michael Jordan, Kobe Bryant, and Dwyane Wade all had major success at the highest level in their careers, but even at that height they had one of the best trainers in the sport in the form of Tim Grover. No one has ever achieved peak performance without a coach or a mentor. If you need help implementing the principles of this book, utilize a coach to fast track your integration. This will decrease the stress and overwhelming feelings you may have as you first start. Book a complimentary thirty-minute session with me or one of my advisors, and let us help you craft a plan that fits your schedule and allows you to navigate your responsibilities.

The one thing that you don't want to do is give up on your dreams, because life as people age comes with more responsibilities which sometimes cause us to give up on our dreams, simply because we're unsure of how to navigate on our own. Let people who have walked in your shoes show you the best way and strategize what works for you.

As a coaching client you'll get access on a one-on-one basis, in addition to resources for many things I've outlined in the marketing section, access to low-cost funding for acquisition of deals, brainstorming sessions, and deal structuring assistance from one of our three advisors.

Don't wait for tomorrow or a job—create one for yourself and others.